The Savvy Woman's Guide to Cars

The Savvy Woman's Guide to Cars

LISA MURR CHAPMAN

BANTAM BOOKS
NEW YORK · TORONTO · LONDON · SYDNEY · AUCKLAND

This book gives the reader a guide to the basics of automobile ownership. Many procedures vary from vehicle to vehicle and from state to state. The reader should refer directly to the automobile's owner's manual and to applicable local laws.

The Savvy Woman's Guide to Cars
A Bantam Book / February 1995

Library of Congress Cataloging-in-Publication Data

Chapman, Lisa Murr.
    The savvy woman's guide to cars / Lisa Murr Chapman.
        p.   cm.
    ISBN 0-553-37408-7
    1. Automobiles—Handbooks, manuals, etc.   2. Women automobile
drivers—Handbooks, manuals, etc.   I. Title.
TL151.C4494   1995
629.222—dc20   94-26891
                                                                 CIP

Published simultaneously in the United States and Canada

PRINTED IN THE UNITED STATES OF AMERICA

FFG   0   9   8   7   6   5   4   3   2   1

This book is dedicated to my father, Ron Murr, who devoted his time and energy to teach and empower me, not only about cars, but about achieving anything I set my mind to.

Contents

Part III Savvy Savings

Part IV Car Buying and Selling

Acknowledgments

Special thanks to my family and friends who helped turn my vision into reality: Kara Livingston, Scott Allen, Mike Milom, Tina Greer, Ron Murr, Dianna Meadows, Jeffrey Hirschfeld, Steve Armistead, Bill Barkley, Billy Flanagan, Roxanne Coats.

And to Brian Tart, my editor at Bantam Books, for his guidance and encouragement.

Introduction

You're busy. The last thing you want to do is hassle over your car. It's time-consuming, frustrating, and expensive. And it seems that everyone is out to rip you off. Take heart. This book is designed to show you how to get control of your car. By keeping this guide in your car, you'll have the power you need to handle almost any situation encountered in a car. Armed with the knowledge in this book, you'll know what to do in case of an emergency, how to protect yourself against over-priced or unnecessary repairs, and how to take care of your automobile investment. You'll be able to improve your car's performance and cut its costs in half. You'll learn the basics of safety, insurance, winter driving, how a car works, and more. Use this guide to buy or sell your car yourself and save your hard-earned money.

This book is about much more than cars, however. It's about confidence and gaining a certain savvy attitude. It's for women who want to feel empowered instead of victimized behind the wheel or under the hood of their car. You never have to feel helpless or powerless because of your car again.

After all, women have traditionally cared for the needs and health of children, family members, and others quite capably. Some people even say that women have an intuitive sense about others' well-being and needs. Certainly the human body is much more complex and fragile than any man-made machine. You can easily apply this intuitive awareness to your automobile. All you need is the basic information to build your foundation. Then trust your senses and approach each new automobile challenge as you might intuitively approach caring for people.

I became savvy about cars through many years of experience and learning from my mistakes. My journey began with the dedicated guidance of my father. His advice and support gave me a strong foundation for venturing out into the male-dominated world of automobiles.

"Make sure your spare tire has plenty of air. . . . Keep the oil full and clean. . . . Always carry a dime with you." These were among my father's gifts to me as a teenager. They've proven to be tremendous seeds of empowerment that have shaped my life more than even he could have known.

The very first thing my father pointed out to me when I got my first car was, "If your tire blows out, you're up a creek if your spare is flat too!" (But as I remember it, he expressed himself more colorfully than that.) "And you need to know how to change the tire yourself." Immediately, we marched out to the driveway to learn how to change a tire, right then and there. It was a sight. I watched him do it as he explained every step very clearly, making sure I followed each move. Then it was my turn. Down to the last detail, I demonstrated my new skill. And I proved that I could do this stuff if I just put my mind to it. Unwittingly, I also learned what's important to keep in the trunk, how to check tire pressure, and how to judge the tread wear and dependability of my tires. All this in only a few minutes! It couldn't be that easy, could it?

I secretly delighted in letting the boys at school know that I could change a tire myself. Somehow, this distinguished me from the girls who couldn't talk cars with them. To this day, that's a fringe benefit of my father's coaching. Conversations nearly always roll around to cars at some point during dinner with a man, or at a party. Surprisingly, most men know much less about automobiles than we might think. When I catch an opportunity to recommend my favorite mechanic, or relate the story of buying my creampuff Jaguar at 20 percent below wholesale, suddenly everyone is interested. They want to learn more and save money, too.

The eighties, a decade of unbridled, conspicuous consumption, is behind us. Carefree yuppie couples who spent megabucks then are probably no longer couples, or at least, no longer carefree. Many are divorced, either living alone or with children. In any case, very few of us are spending money the way we used to.

So, too, went the era of female helplessness and dependency. We are a new generation of women in charge. Our choices are increasingly directed by our dreams and desires in every facet of our lives. We are forging the lead in our fitness, family management, home ownership, careers, and financial decisions. My father is quite the Renaissance man in that regard. Instead of doing everything for me, he had the vision to give me the ability and confidence to go after what I wanted myself. For many women, a missing link has been in the automobile arena. There is no good reason for this to continue. Women are very capable of handling automobile challenges, just as they can handle any other challenging situation. This book gives you the information you need to bridge the gap and let yourself into the automobile arena.

Somewhat like the story of the Velveteen Rabbit, becoming savvy doesn't happen all at once. You slowly, deliberately become savvy. That's part of the fun. You don't have to know everything right away. Savvy isn't necessarily knowing how to fix a car, or even knowing what's wrong with it. Savvy is knowing just enough to handle your car and its challenges appropriately. Savvy means you are likely to spend less money and feel less intimidated than you used to. And once you are savvy you can't become unsavvy again. You'll have it forever. My father gets the credit for helping me understand all about it, just as the Velveteen Rabbit learned from the Skin Horse. A small investment of time now will pay off for years in lower car costs, more money saved, far fewer headaches, and most .

important, a confidence and security in your own ability to handle all aspects of a car.

Oil was the one fundamental aspect of car ownership that became a critical rite of passage presented by my father. Not because we lived in Houston, Texas, but rather because he didn't want me to burn up the engine. This is the kind of thing that boys pick up from other boys. Girls, on the other hand, generally have very limited exposure to a discussion of the consequences of excessive oil consumption by an automobile. So he made sure that I understood. "Keep the oil full and clean. Check it every other time you fill your gas tank. Have the oil and oil filter changed every three thousand miles." As you might suspect, we journeyed back out to the driveway to learn how to check it. From that moment on, I was responsible for keeping track of it. If I forgot, I risked engine damage *and* my father's ire. On my way out the door he'd often quiz me, "How's the oil in your car?" If I didn't know, I couldn't bluff because he'd follow right behind me insisting, "How about we just check it real quick to be sure?" That always preceded a reiteration of how important it is to keep the oil full and clean. If you don't, you'll have a real emergency on your hands.

And so, before my father ever allowed me to drive away, I answered the final question, "Do you have a dime?" Back then, a call from a pay phone cost only a dime. By the time I have children old enough to drive off for the evening, I'll probably be asking, "Is your car phone working?" My father made sure that if I had any problems, I could deal with them proactively, by either taking care of them myself or calling the appropriate person for help. Having a dime was very empowering in case of an emergency.

Every savvy woman has an emergency plan. Emergencies happen. But they don't have to be overwhelming, and they don't have to wipe out your savings. I learned this the hard way when I had transmission problems. Transmission repair is major league—high cost, high hassle. Quite honestly, I earned my major league savvy title after falling victim to a typical scam. Unfortunately, many of us do. Feeling cheated and mistreated, we are motivated to take action and arm ourselves with the information we need to prevent similar experiences in the future. This particular transmission repair was one of the catalysts that inspired me to write this book. Originally quoted at $350, my transmission repair cost over $1,900 and was never satisfactorily completed. And I never received restitution.

These types of scams are more prevalent than people realize. Initially, I had no idea that there are so many ways to render the naive car consumer virtually helpless, at the complete mercy of the repair shop. My transmission repair was a very expensive lesson that can save everyone lots of money and grief. (More about how to do that in Chapter 6.) After two years of trying in vain to find an equitable resolution, I was in a real quandary. How could I sell this problem car to an unsuspecting individual and live with my conscience? Ultimately, I found a dealer who was willing to take it "as is." I realized a loss of another $2,000 and was inducted into the majors.

After sharing this story with family and friends, it became all too clear that this experience was far from unique. However, most people hesitate to discuss similar incidents because they are often annoyed with themselves and embarrassed to admit them. This, perhaps, is one benefit of being female in the automobile world. After all, we aren't expected to know these things. Well, that time has passed.

The Department of Transportation reports that 53 percent of all auto repair costs are unnecessary. Consumer rights activist Ralph Nader estimates this cost at $40 billion annually in the U.S. alone. The stories I've heard about auto repair scams make me mad enough to spit nails. The worst of them are a result of outright fraud. A scam-artist mechanic might drop a seltzer tablet into your battery to create an overflow. Or a squirt of oil in a strategic place will give you the impression that a seal has broken, if not something much more costly. Honest, hardworking people who can barely scrape enough money together to pay their bills are most often the unsuspecting victims. Single mothers who rely upon their automobile for transportation every day to earn a living and keep their families together are, sadly, the most vulnerable and hardest hit. Financial distress due to automobile scams has often ruined their credit and left them without any transportation, not to mention the mental anguish that it causes victims. Because women are believed to have less knowledge and experience in the world of cars, scammers are bolder and take greater liberties with them. They tend to view women as uninformed and vulnerable victims who aren't able to distinguish reasonable from unreasonable repair costs and service. But information is power.

Contrary to popular belief, car maintenance, repairs, sales, and purchases are not as difficult as raising children, climbing the corporate ladder, or juggling a career and family. Becoming car savvy takes only the desire to empower yourself and a small bit of effort. The problem was that this information has never been readily available in a concise, comprehensive, user-friendly format for the female consumer. When this fact dawned on me, I knew that women everywhere could save a lot of time, money, and heartache by reading a book to become savvy about their cars. More than 81 million American women were licensed drivers in 1990. More than 25 million of them relied upon transportation in order to work and support dependents. More than 44 percent of all new car buyers in 1990 were female, while 60 percent of all Toyota buyers in 1992 were female. Women roughly spend an astounding $65 billion every year on cars. They are fast becoming the majority of the car-buying decision makers and purchasers. Yet, as always, we often feel powerless over our cars and victimized by car scams.

Did you know that most people buy about 15 cars in their lifetime and spend about $325,000? Just by following the few simple steps outlined in these pages, you can cut your car costs by half or more. After my transmission fiasco, I was bound and determined to learn the "secrets" of the car business and use them to buy a very nice, reliable car that met my needs and cost wholesale or less. Ha! Even my closest friends were skeptical. But their cynicism only served to strengthen my resolve. Where there's a will, there's a way.

Maneuvering through the bewildering maze of the used car business is treacherous if you're not familiar with the land mines. Since I wasn't, I began at the beginning. For me, that meant the library. A wealth of information was waiting right there, in books and periodicals written almost exclusively by men and for men. *Consumer Reports* and a number of others were quite helpful with evaluations and comparisons of vehicles in distinct categories. After delving into them and narrowing down the categories to those that most appealed to me and met my needs, I began to comparison shop in the local classifieds. Prices vary tremendously, and for good reasons: make, model, year, options, mileage, and condition are but a few of the variables that affect the market value of each car. No two used cars are identical. For this reason, price guides such as the NADA (National Automobile Dealers Association) book are indispensable. Although they certainly don't guarantee that a car you're considering is a good value if it falls within NADA guidelines, it's a good bet that if you pay more for the car, you are most likely overpaying.

Next, I graduated to browsing on car lots, but not really shopping, since I had no intention of buying until I learned the secrets. Shopping entails negotiating. This is how you get the best experience and learn from your mistakes. Only it's much easier because you aren't buying, so you don't have to pay for your mistakes for years to come! Several times I spotted a lonely used car lot managed by an older gentleman. After warming up to him and admitting that I was not a buyer but a researcher, I asked for advice. These types of gentlemen were usually proud to share their knowledge of the business with me. I learned from the inside how the business works; this is certainly the most savvy perspective.

The more I learned about cars and how the automobile business works, the more convinced I became that women were generally treated in an inferior manner in the car world. Female car buyers have needs that may be very different from their male counterparts. For instance, women want to feel secure in their cars. Reliability and safety are major factors. In spite of this, the automobile industry as a whole has been slow to respond to women's needs. Only 6 percent of the 170,000 car salespeople in the United States are female. Less than half of the new-car dealerships employ even one female salesperson.

A recent survey conducted by a major national magazine reports that 62 percent of the female respondents believe they are treated worse than men as car buyers. Edward Lapham, executive editor of *Automotive News*, confirms that "women are still not being taken seriously as a customer. When women are treated badly, or stupidly, they leave." Women deserve to be understood without feeling intimidated, overwhelmed, or pressured. I became dedicated to getting involved and doing something about it.

I firmly believe that women can and should have access to dependable, affordable, and stylish cars at a fair price without feeling mistreated. As I discussed my convictions and the unmet needs I identified, women everywhere enthusiastically agreed. As a result, I rallied the talents and resources of a few key car and business associates to open Motorcars of Brentwood, a car dealership in Middle Tennessee dedicated to empowering women with information and offering solid values in preowned cars. The response from the community and the press has exceeded my hopes. And working with women to help them lower their car expenses and take charge of managing their cars has been exciting and tremendously rewarding.

As a result of this experience, *The Savvy Woman's Guide to Cars* can offer you what you need most to demystify the overwhelming maze of confusion and can enable you to make informed automobile decisions. Remember, you don't have to know everything right away, and there is no need to memorize the details. Trying to learn everything about cars would be a frustrating and unrealistic chore. This book will not teach you how to become a car doctor, just how your car got sick and what to do about it. It will not teach you how to become an auto mechanic, just how to avoid being ripped off by one. To become car savvy, you need only become aware of typical problems and how to approach them effectively. Beyond that, a constructive approach to problem solving is the key to handling successfully any new automobile challenge. Familiarize yourself with the contents of this book and where to find key information. Then keep it in your car to serve as a quick reference when you need it most.

PART I

Car Basics and Safety

I

The Six Savvy
Essentials

If you've never touched the workings of a car, you've got to
start somewhere, and learning how to handle the following six
simple tasks is the perfect place. They take only minutes to
learn and promise to eliminate untold expense and frustration.
They are the basics of car maintenance: filling your gas tank;
changing a flat tire; checking tire pressure; jump-starting your
car; checking and adding oil; and checking your radiator fluid.
They are the foundation of being a savvy car owner and the
first steps to empowerment. You will be faced with them most
often. With these six savvy essentials, you will begin to take
control of your car. A knowledgeable friend or mechanic can
walk you through them the first time. So go ahead and just do it
now, *before* you're in a bind. You'll be well on your way to
taking charge. After you do these once, you'll find that it's like
riding a bike . . . you never forget how.

Number 1: How to Fill Your Gas Tank

You can save more than $100 a year by filling your own gas
tank, because service stations charge up to ten cents a gallon

more at full-service pumps. You are throwing away money by going to the full-service pump all the time. The full-service pump should be a luxury rather than a necessity. Every woman should be able to pump her own gas—it's easy to do and is a fundamental step toward empowering yourself within the car world. The following instructions are a basic guideline for filling your gas tank, and are mainly to reinforce how simple and straightforward this activity is. If you've never filled your own tank before, you may want to ask an attendant at your local gas station to show you how their pump operates so you will be familiar with the pump and nozzle when you do it alone.

1. Pull up to the pump (on the gas-cap side of your car) for the appropriate type of gasoline for your car.
2. Remove your gas cap. You may need to pull a release lever inside your car to gain access to the gas cap.
3. Remove the nozzle from the pump and place it deep into your tank. Push the nozzle into the tank as far as it can go.
4. Move the handle to the "on" position or press the "start" button. This should clear the pump to start at $0.00.
5. Pull the trigger on the nozzle to start the flow of gas. Hold it until it clicks off when your tank is full. If it clicks before your tank is full, it means the nozzle is not inserted correctly. Readjust the nozzle in the tank and pull the trigger again.
6. Return the nozzle to the pump.
7. Replace your gas cap.
8. Pay the attendant the amount shown in the pump window.

Number 2: How to Change a Flat Tire

Having a flat tire can be a disheartening experience and a nasty job, unless you know how to do it right. Here's how:

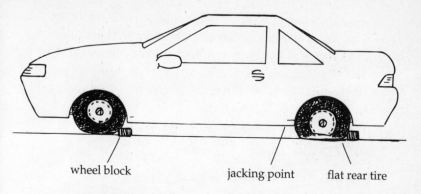

Figure 1. Wheel blocks and jacking point: side view

1. BEFORE YOU JACK UP YOUR CAR:

- Park on level ground off the road.
- Put your car in park or, if it is a standard, leave it in first gear so it cannot roll.
- Put the emergency brake on.
- Put your emergency flashers on.

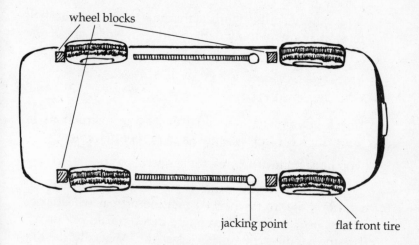

Figure 2. Wheel blocks and jacking point: bottom view

- Block the wheels to prevent rolling. Use rocks, bricks, boards, or any heavy object that can be wedged under the tire. This will help prevent the car from moving once it is jacked up.
- Take out your spare tire.

2. REMOVE THE HUBCAP AND LOOSEN THE LUG NUTS.

To remove the hubcap:

- Use a screwdriver to pry the hubcap off the wheel as you would open a can of paint. You may need a special wrench to unlock the hubcap.
- Use the hubcap as a bowl to hold the lug nuts while you change the tire.

To loosen the lug nuts:

- Use your lug wrench.
- If the lug nut has an *L* on it, turn clockwise to loosen it.
- If it has nothing or an *R* on it, turn counterclockwise to loosen it.
- *Loosen* the lug nuts slightly at this time to ensure equal bolt tension and avoid any damage to your tire's rim or the wheel well. Don't remove them yet.

3. JACK UP YOUR CAR.

- Check your owner's manual or jacking instructions in your trunk for jack assembly and proper placement.

If you have no instructions, remember:

- Position the jack under the car frame or the large bar that supports the front wheel suspension or rear wheel axle.
- Never use a support that might bend, break, or "give."
- Use the handle to pump the jack's "lift." When the flat tire clears the ground, you can stop.

Figure 3. Remove the hubcap

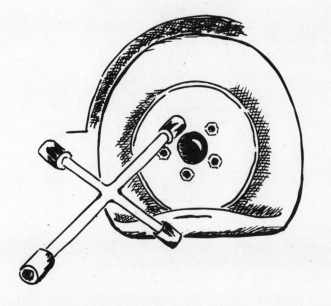

Figure 4. Loosen the lug nuts

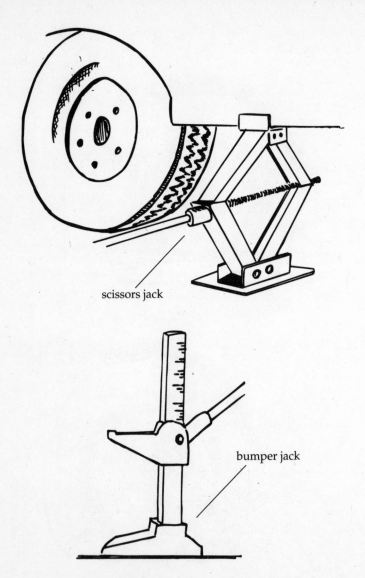

scissors jack

bumper jack

Figure 5. Position the jack

- Make sure the car is secure, not wobbly. If it is wobbly, lower the car and reposition the jack to provide more support. You may need to move the car to more stable terrain.
- *Never* get under a car that is jacked up.

4. CHANGE THE TIRE.

- Remove the lug nuts (that were just loosened in Step 2) and place them in your hubcap on the ground.
- Remove the wheel by pulling it toward yourself and get it out of the way.
- Lift the spare onto the lug bolts, replacing the flat you just removed.

Figure 6. Remove the wheel

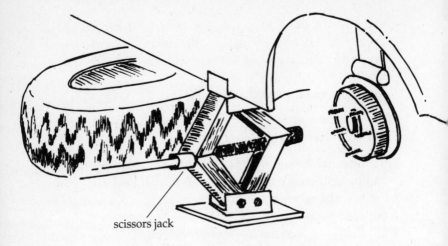

scissors jack

Figure 7.

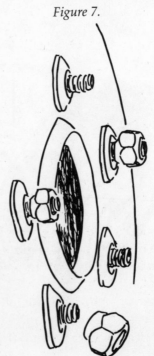

Figure 8. Replace the lug nuts after mounting spare tire

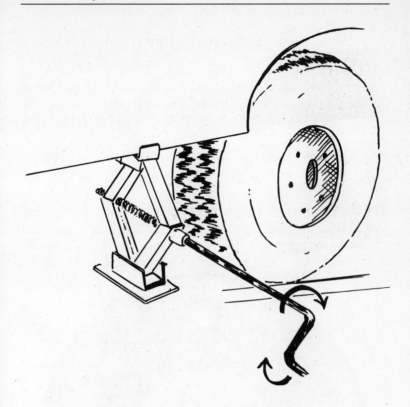

Figure 9. Lower the car with the jack

- Replace the lug nuts and tighten all of them snugly in the same order you loosened them so that the wheel is secure. Turn them the opposite way you did in Step 2.
- Lower the car with the jack until the tire is touching the ground but not supporting the car's full weight.
- Tighten the lug nuts with the lug wrench. Get them tight enough to be sure they won't come loose.
- Put the hubcap in the trunk for now. You can replace it once the flat is fixed.
- Put your flat tire and tools away in the trunk.
- Remove the wheel blocks.

5. REMEMBER TO HAVE YOUR TIRE FIXED AS SOON AS POSSIBLE.

The spare may be a small "space saver," which is not meant for speeds over 30 mph or for traveling over 50 miles.

Number 3: How to Check Tire Pressure and Add Air

Correct tire pressure has a direct impact on your safety, comfort, and car expenses. By keeping your tires inflated to their recommended pressure, you will enhance your car's handling

Figure 10. How to read a tire

and performance as well as help to avoid potentially dangerous blowouts. You may save up to $100 a year as a result of improved fuel efficiency, and the useful life of your tires may be extended for years. Follow these tips:

Check tires "cold"—before you've driven three miles.

Tire pressure is measured in pounds per square inch (psi).

The correct psi for your tires should be noted on the outside of the tire itself, or on the sticker inside the driver's doorjamb, or on the glove compartment door.

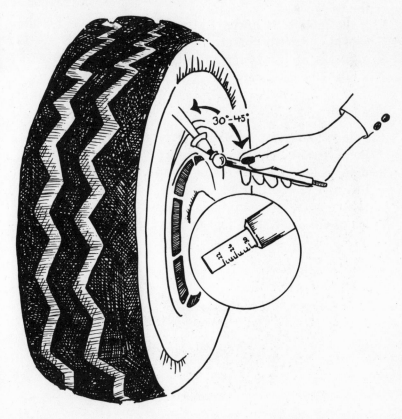

Figure 11. Checking the pressure

Use your tire gauge to check your psi:

1. Remove the valve cap that covers the valve leading to the tire.
2. Press the gauge onto the valve until the hissing sound stops. This "hissing" is air leaving the tire. Although it can be distracting, it does not hurt the tire to let a small amount of air out.
3. The last number showing on the pop-out slide ruler should match your recommended psi.
4. If the number is higher, let air out by pressing the pin in the tire valve.
5. If the number is lower, add air. Service stations usually provide air free of charge.
6. Recheck until your psi is correct.
7. Replace the valve cap.

To add air:

1. Pull up to the air pump at the service station.
2. Remove the valve cap.
3. Remove the hose from the air pump and press the end onto the valve to insert air into your tire.
4. Use your tire gauge to check your psi.
5. When you're finished, replace the valve cap.

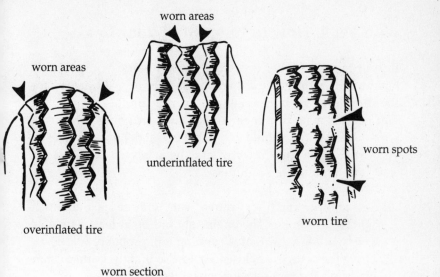

worn areas

underinflated tire

worn areas

overinflated tire

worn spots

worn tire

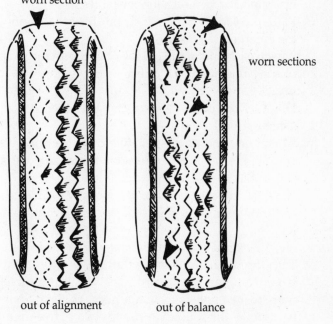

worn section

out of alignment

worn sections

out of balance

Figure 12. Improper tire wear to look out for

Number 4: How to Jump-Start Your Car

If your lights or other accessories won't work, you probably have a dead battery. Batteries can usually be revived, at least for the short term, by borrowing power from another vehicle. All you need is a set of jumper cables and a running car with a strong battery. You should *always* have a set of jumper cables in your trunk. (See page 52 for what to have in your car.) You can start it in less than ten minutes:

1. Use another car (the "source" car) with at least as much voltage as yours. (The engine should be at least as big as yours, but any car that is running will probably work.)
2. Drive the source car close to yours, so that the batteries can be connected by your jumper cables.
3. Place the cars in park or neutral. Turn the engines off. Put the emergency brakes on.
4. Attach each end of the positive cable with the red clips *only* to the *positive terminal* of each car's battery ("+"). Red = positive.
5. Don't let the cable clips touch each other. It could create some fireworks.
6. Attach one end of the negative cable with the black clips *only* to the *negative terminal* of the source car's battery ("−"). Black = negative.
7. Connect the other end of the negative cable to exposed metal of your car's engine, keeping it away from the battery.
8. Start the source car, and have the driver idle fast.
9. Turn the key in your car to start it.
10. If your engine won't turn over, check the cable connections to be sure you have a good contact. Sometimes it helps to let the source car run for two to five minutes, then try again.
11. After your car starts, turn off the source car.

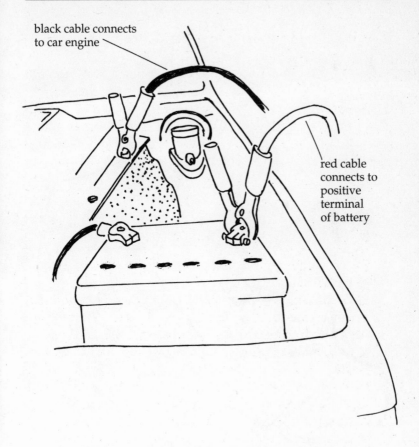

black cable connects
to car engine

red cable
connects to
positive
terminal
of battery

Figure 13. Connecting jumper cables to dead car

12. If your car still won't start, it's best to call AAA for a tow. You don't want to risk damaging your starter (which is quite expensive to replace). Turn off the source car.
13. Disconnect the black cables first.
14. If your alternator light stays on when your car is running, the problem probably isn't your battery. Have your mechanic check it. (See Chapter 6 on finding a good mechanic.)

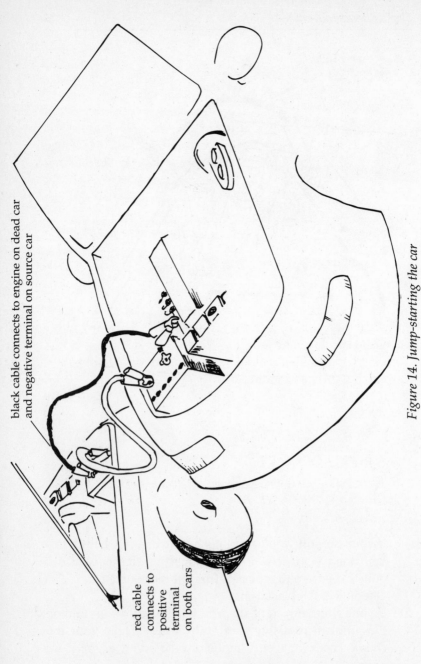

black cable connects to engine on dead car and negative terminal on source car

red cable connects to positive terminal on both cars

Figure 14. Jump-starting the car

Number 5: How to Check and Add Oil

Keeping your oil full and clean are the two most important things you can do to ensure that your car stays as healthy as possible. It takes very little time to check your oil when you stop for gas, and it could save you thousands of dollars. If you wait until your oil light goes on to check and add oil you've probably already done significant damage to your engine, which will cost you *big* bucks to repair.

To prevent that kind of expense, check your oil each time you go on a trip. Oil should be checked every 3,000 miles, as a general rule. (See page 98 for Quick Checklist and Maintenance Record.) Here's how:

1. Park on level ground and turn off the engine.
2. Locate the metal ring of the oil dipstick. It is located in the engine and is usually easy to reach. To find it on your car, refer to your owner's manual. If it's not clear to you, have a service station attendant point it out.
3. Pull out the dipstick and wipe it free of oil with a clean, soft cloth.
4. Push it back in all the way. Wait a few seconds and pull it straight back out.
5. "Read" the oil on the stick by noting where the oil ends relative to the dipstick markings. If "add" is clearly visible, add oil now. It will probably take a quart to reach the "full" mark on the dipstick.

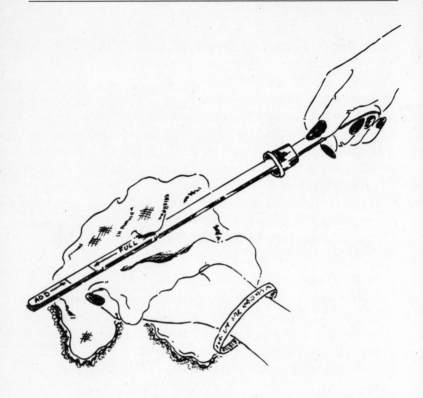

Figure 15. Oil dipstick

When your car is a half to one quart low, you need to add oil.
It's easy:

1. Turn off your engine.
2. Unscrew the oil cap and pour the oil into the oil-fill hole. You
   may need a funnel or pouring spout.
3. Be sure to replace the oil cap.
4. Wait a few minutes for it to settle and check the oil again.

By checking your oil frequently, you will become familiar with
your engine's "appetite" for more oil. You can gauge it roughly
by the number of miles you drive before it needs more.

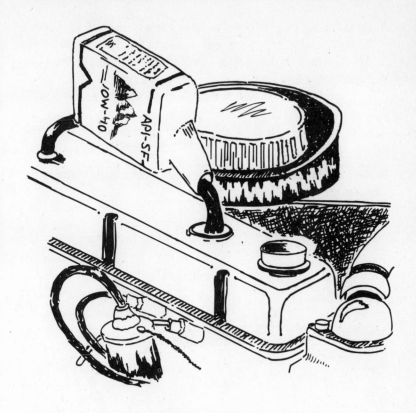

Figure 16. Adding oil

Number 6: How to Check Your Radiator and Add Coolant

Your engine temperature can get as hot as 5,000° F. If you don't have enough coolant in your car, it will overheat and leave you stranded on the roadside. Check your radiator every month, every time you check your oil, or at least every 3,000 miles. Determine an interval that works for you and be consistent. Here's how:

1. Find the radiator coolant recovery reservoir (usually a plastic tank near the radiator and connected to it by a hose). If it's not clear to you, have a service station attendant point it out.
2. "Read" the level on the side of the reservoir.
   - If your engine is hot, the coolant should be at the hot fill mark.
   - If your engine is cold, the coolant should be at the cold fill mark.
3. Add coolant to the reservoir in a 50/50 mix with water to the appropriate mark.

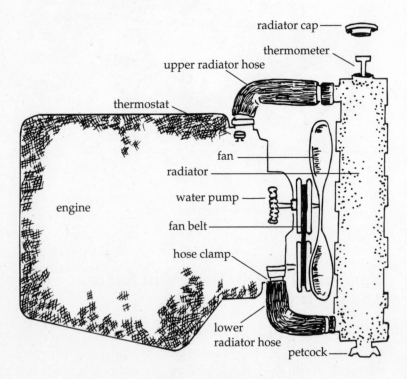

Figure 17. Radiator

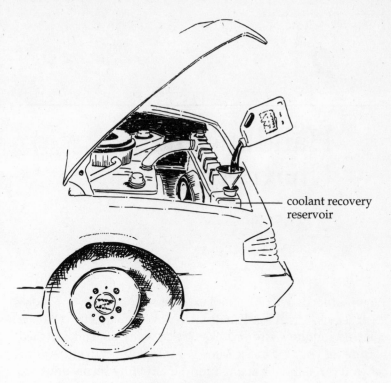

coolant recovery reservoir

Figure 18. Adding coolant

Note: Do not attempt to open the radiator cap when it is hot. The pressure and steam of a hot radiator could badly burn you. While it's hot, add to the coolant reservoir *only*, or wait for it to cool down.

2

Handling the Unexpected

When someone we care about exhibits strange behavior, looks ill, or seems hurt, it's only natural to pull them quietly off to the side and inquire, "Are you okay?" It's really not so farfetched to think of your car in the same way. As you get to know your car, you can tell if it's acting funny, if anything seems unusual, or if it doesn't sound right, smell right, look right, feel right, or perform right.

This chapter alerts you to many of the typical symptoms that your car may exhibit and that you'll identify just by tuning in to your senses. Glance through these now, so you'll know what to be aware of. When you detect a problem, pay attention to it *right away*, before it gets more complicated and costly (it certainly will if you let it go). Trust your senses. Use your intuitive skills. If you suspect something is wrong, it probably is. Take it right in for a diagnosis by a qualified mechanic. (Also see Chapter 6 to Get It Fixed Right the First Time for a Fair Price.)

By proactively managing the health of your car, you'll save yourself a lot of time, money, and frustration. Don't let your car's simple cold turn into a more painful, lingering disease.

If Your Car Won't Start

This usually happens at the most frustrating times: you're running late, someone's waiting for you, or it's snowing. Depending upon the circumstances and your car's symptoms, a variety of things may help. By identifying the source of the problem before you take it to a mechanic, you will take a very important step toward protecting yourself against car scams. Here's a quick reference to give you some direction.

Common Symptoms	Possible Reason(s)	What to Do
Nothing happens when you turn the key	Dead battery	Jump-start (see page 26)
	Dirty or loose battery cable connections	Have cables cleaned, replaced, or tightened* Call AAA
Only a clicking noise when you turn the key	Usually a dead battery	Jump-start
	Loose starter or battery cables	Secure starter wiring connection or replace wiring*
	Dirty cable connection	Clean and secure cable connections* Call AAA
Tough to start on a cold morning	May be ice in gas line or gas tank	In winter, add a can of Heet to your gas tank to help prevent this
	Choke may be malfunctioning	Call AAA or adjust the choke's butterfly valve to remain closed when cold*

Common Symptoms	Possible Reason(s)	What to Do
Car starts and dies or is slow to warm up	Idle may be set too low	Call AAA or adjust the idle.* For fuel-injected cars, get a mechanic to do this
Car cranks but won't start	Distributor cap wear or moisture	Call AAA
	Inadequate fuel supply to the carburetor	Call AAA
	Out of gas	Add two gallons
Won't start on rainy days	Distributor cap may be damp inside	Call AAA or use mechanic's solvent to evaporate the water*

* Many of these solutions can be performed by a knowledgeable layperson or an AAA representative. Due to their relatively infrequent occurrence, detailed instructions are not included in this text.

If Warning Lights Go On While You're Driving

If this happens, you must treat it as an emergency. Follow the instructions on page 37 and consult the appropriate chapter in this book so you will know what is wrong with the car and avoid getting scammed.

Warning Light	*What to Do*
Oil:	*Stop immediately.* Pull off to the shoulder, turn your emergency flashers on, and turn off the engine. Call AAA or a tow truck. Do not start the engine until the problem has been solved. If you ignore this warning it may cost you a new engine, which means megabucks!
Water temperature:	*Stop immediately.* Let the engine cool down. See page 38 for If Your Car Overheats or call AAA if you do not have water with you to fill the car. Ignoring this may also cost you a new engine.
Check engine:	Stop immediately. Call for help. Check your owner's manual to find out what this light means for your car. This light can mean different things, but ignoring it may also cost you a new engine.
Charging system:	You may drive only a short distance to the nearest service station. Make sure you don't drive more than a couple miles, however, and don't stop and restart your car. See page 74 for more information related to creating the car's power.
Brakes:	You may drive only a short distance to the nearest service station. You're probably losing brake fluid. Try not to use your brakes a lot. If this is not possible, stop immediately and call AAA. See page 90 for more information related to controlling the power.
Gas:	You may drive only a short distance to the nearest service station. The amount of fuel left in the tank is minimal when the light appears and also varies from car to car. But chances are, you won't make it more than a few miles.

If Your Car Overheats

Overheating is not a disease in your car. It is a symptom of a disease, just as it is with our own bodies. Overheating is like a nagging cough or a sore throat that signals you to a more dangerous problem, like bronchitis or pneumonia. You will first detect overheating by watching the water temperature indicator on your dashboard. It's best by far to deal with this symptom immediately. Don't try to drive to the nearest service station.

WHEN YOU FIRST SUSPECT OVERHEATING:

1. Turn off your air conditioner and open your windows.
2. Turn on the heater and fan (this diverts the heat away from the engine).
3. Shift into neutral and rev the engine.
4. Don't ride your brakes.

IF IT BOILS OVER (you will notice steam rising from under the hood):

1. Drive immediately to the shoulder.
2. Turn on your emergency flashers.
3. Shut off the car.
4. Open the hood.
5. Look for a hole in the radiator hose. (It can be temporarily "fixed" with duct tape.) (See page 31 for How to Check Your Radiator and Add Coolant.)
6. Don't open the radiator cap when it's hot.
7. Add water or coolant to the reservoir *only*.
8. After adding water or coolant, try to drive it again.

If it continues to overheat call AAA for help or a tow to your mechanic. There could be a variety of reasons for this overheating, including: Plugged or leaking radiator, slipping fan belt or no fan belt, collapsed radiator hose, low oil level (see page 29 for How to Check and Add Oil), or faulty thermostat. Repair time and costs may vary widely with these problems. Refer to page 117 to Get It Fixed Right the First Time for a Fair Price.

If Your Car Runs Out of Gas

Just for the record, running out of gas is hard on your car's engine and may cost you time and money. It should be avoided at all costs.

But, if you do run out of gas, your car will probably sputter, jerk, and lose engine power. When this happens, your power steering and power brakes will go out. This is a dangerous situation. Get to the roadside immediately. Leave the car in gear or in neutral so you can steer the car to safety. Once safely on the side of the road, turn the key to the "off" position and turn on your emergency flashers. Call AAA or take your empty gas can to the nearest service station. Your funnel will be helpful for putting gas into your gas tank. You should never keep a spare can of gas in your car. It could ignite upon impact in an accident.

Because there was no gas going to the engine when you were pumping the gas pedal while trying to start your car, your fuel line has now filled with air. After putting some gas into your tank, pump the gas pedal ten to twelve times before trying to turn the ignition. It may take several attempts to start your engine because the gasoline must make its way through the empty fuel lines. If you are still unable to start the car, it's best to call AAA or a qualified mechanic for a diagnosis.

If You Lock Yourself Out

This happens to just about everyone, sooner or later. When it does, you've joined the millions of us who've become a little bit savvier through the experience. Although you may be frustrated, you have several options for getting into your car. If you can get a simple wire coat hanger, you may be able to use it to get into the window, hook the door lock to pull it up, and unlock the door. This works only with golf-tee-shaped door lock buttons. First, straighten the coat hanger so that it is long enough to reach the button. Make a V-shaped hook on the end strong enough to catch the button and pull it up. Insert the hook end between the window and the rubber molding, shoving it into the car toward the button. When you can hook the button, pull up to unlock it. Older model cars may be easier to hook. In fact, this may not be possible with most newer models.

Your dealer always keeps your car's key code for five years after you purchase it. Even if you move away, a dealer in your area will be sent out with a key for a nominal charge (under ten dollars). If that fails, and you can't get in touch with your dealer, call AAA. Their tow truck drivers carry a tool called a Slim-Jim just for this event. As a member, you will not be charged for this service.

If you are desperate, call a locksmith, but be prepared to prove you own the car and to pay immediately. If you are *really* desperate, your last resort may be to break a window, preferably a passenger-side wing window or rear window, which are safer to break and less expensive to replace. If duct tape or masking tape is available, covering the window with tape before breaking it will help prevent shattered glass from spraying into the car.

Figuring Out When You Might Have Car Trouble

As I mentioned in the introduction, trust your senses when dealing with your car. You do it all the time at home with your family, with your friends, and on the job. It comes quite naturally when you are in tune with your environment. Awareness is the most important step toward catching potential problems early and saving money, time, and frustration. If anything sounds, smells, looks, or feels peculiar, check it out right away. Here are a few common maladies to look out for:

If You Hear . . .

If you hear:	*Possible cause:*	*Possible solution:*
Thumping tires	Flat tire	See page 14 for How to Change a Flat Tire
	Badly worn tire	Check for excessive wear and change tires if needed
Pings or knocks	Wrong gas—octane too low	Fill your tank with a higher octane gas
	Dirty air filter	Replace air filter (auto parts stores or your mechanic can show you how, for little to no charge)
	Carburetor setting or tune-up needed	Have your mechanic check it

If you hear:	Possible cause:	Possible solution:
Squealing under the hood, especially when you accelerate	Loose belt on: • cooling fan • air conditioner • alternator • power steering	Have a mechanic check it immediately before it causes more serious damage or overheating
Loud exhaust	Muffler or exhaust pipe defect	Have a certified exhaust systems mechanic check it; diverted carbon monoxide could be dangerous
Squealing tires around corners	Underinflated tires	See page 22 for How to Check Tire Pressure and Add Air
	Bald or excessively worn tires	Replace your tires before they blow out or cause an accident
Squealing or grinding when you brake	Worn brake pads or shoes	Have brakes checked by a mechanic immediately; this can be dangerous and expensive
Hissing under the hood	Radiator or hose leak	Stop immediately before it overheats. Check under your hood; you may need to call AAA

If you hear:	Possible cause:	Possible solution:
Clunking	Low transmission fluid	Check the fluid level
	Universal joint or rear differential malfunction	Have a good mechanic check it very soon
Sputtering	Engine may not be getting enough fuel due to: • bad fuel pump • clogged fuel filter • carburetor trouble • clogged fuel injector nozzles	Have a mechanic check it out

If You Smell . . .

If you smell:	Possible cause:	Possible solution:
Something burning from under your hood	Left your emergency brake on	Release the brake all the way
	Extremely low level of oil	Check oil level and check engine parts for signs of an oil leak
	Melting hoses	If nothing's visible, call AAA or have a mechanic check it out
	Tire problems such as a locked wheel or brake resistance	Pull off the road and let them cool down, or call AAA

If you smell:	Possible cause:	Possible solution:
	Short-circuited electrical system	Pull off immediately and call AAA
	Fuel leak fire	Pull over and carefully open the hood. If there is a fire, *do not* use water, use a fire extinguisher, sand, or dirt
Gas fumes	Leak in fuel line, carburetor, or fuel tank	Pull over and turn off the engine
"Rotten eggs"	Catalytic converter may be sending the wrong fuel mixture to the engine	Have your mechanic adjust the carburetor

If You See . . .

If you see:	Possible cause:	Possible solution:
Yellow-green puddles under your parked car	Leaking coolant from a burst or detached hose	Temporarily tape or clamp it to get it to your mechanic (see page 31 on radiators and coolants)
Brownish black spots under your parked car	If it's between the rear wheels, it may be leaking rear-axle/ differential fluid	Drive immediately to your nearest mechanic

If you see:	Possible cause:	Possible solution:
	If it's in the front, it may be leaking oil	Check and fill your oil. Then have your mechanic check it for leaks
Reddish fluid spots under your parked car	Leaking automatic transmission fluid or power steering fluid	Check the fluid levels and/or take it to your mechanic
Water spots under your parked car	Usually no problem. Normal air conditioner use causes water condensation drips	Usually none needed
Black smoke spews out of the tail pipe when you start the car	Malfunctioning carburetor or automatic choke	Consult your mechanic
A bulge in the tire	Separated tread	Consult your mechanic before you have a blowout
Tires are wearing out faster in the middle	Overinflated tires	Check tire pressure and adjust to recommended psi
Tires are wearing out faster on one side	Underinflated tires	Check tire pressure and adjust to recommended psi
	Wheels are out of alignment	Have them checked by a professional —car may need alignment

If you see:	*Possible cause:*	*Possible solution:*
Tires wearing faster in center of tread	Underinflated	Check pressure, possibly add air
Tires wearing faster on both sides	Overinflated	Check pressure, possibly let air out
One tire always needs more air	Slow leak in that tire or air valve	Examine the tire for a puncture or embedded object, then have it checked by a professional

If You Feel . . .

If you feel:	*Possible cause:*	*Possible solution:*
Difficulty starting after car sits awhile	Fouled spark plugs	Replace spark plugs (your mechanic should do this)
	Malfunctioning automatic choke	Consult your mechanic
Backfiring when you start it	Malfunction of your emissions system or worn distributor points	Consult your mechanic
Your steering gets stiff	Stalled car	Restart your engine
	Power steering fluid leak or broken belt	Pull into the nearest service station or pull over and call AAA

If you feel:	Possible cause:	Possible solution:
Your steering gets loose	Damaged or badly worn steering component or wheel bearings	Consult your mechanic immediately
The car pulls to the right or left	Front wheels may be out of alignment	Have them aligned soon to avoid excessive tire wear
The steering wheel shakes or shimmies	Front wheels may be out of balance	Have your wheels balanced by a mechanic
Your automatic transmission won't move when you put it in drive gear	Parking brake may be on Very low transmission fluid	Release it all the way Check the fluid level and add fluid, then have a *reputable* transmission specialist check it out
Your automatic transmission shifts oddly (i.e., rough, jerky, slipping, etc.)	Low transmission fluid Parts in your transmission may need adjustment, repair, or replacement	Check fluid level and add fluid if necessary Have a reputable transmission specialist check it out

If you feel:	*Possible cause:*	*Possible solution:*
Your clutch sticks, it's hard to change gears, or the clutch rattles in gear	Worn or faulty transmission parts or clutch	Have a reputable transmission specialist check it out
Your brake pedal goes almost to the floor before it responds	Low brake fluid	Get to a service station immediately or pull over and call AAA
You have to pump the brakes to get the car to stop	Low brake fluid	Check fluid levels and add fluid if necessary
	Air in the brake lines or leaking master cylinder	Consult your mechanic immediately
The car is unusually bumpy	Worn shock absorbers	Consult your mechanic
Other engine or performance problems, including: • rough idling • missing (misfiring) • hesitation • sluggishness • stalling • surging • poor fuel economy • dieseling (runs after you turn it off)	Many varied possible causes	Consult your mechanic soon, so it doesn't become a bigger problem

3

Better Safe Than Sorry

Better safe than sorry. Who can argue with that? But it's a fact that if you have a car, drive one, or ride in one, you face the risk of a car-related crime or injury every single day. By knowing what to do and then doing it, you will take an active role in substantially lowering these risks.

According to the nonprofit Crime Prevention League, a car is stolen every 26 seconds in the United States. Two out of every three Americans will be injured in a car accident sometime in their lives. Automobile accidents are the number one cause of death through age 40, while more than 2 million people suffer disabling injuries every year. By simply using seat belts, air bags, adhering to the 55 mph speed limit, and avoiding alcohol before driving, your risk of fatal injury in a car accident drops by almost half.

These simple precautions are only the beginning. This chapter will also help prepare you for emergencies, protect you against car crimes, and guard your children from harm. Savvy women do these things.

Be Savvy: How to Avoid Car Crimes

Car crimes against women have escalated at an alarming rate. Urban drivers were the first to experience such assaults, and now suburban and even rural drivers must beware. Car crimes may be avoided by taking simple precautions that can easily become second nature and part of your daily routine. Awareness is the first step toward taking control.

Crimes against female drivers are many. Some of the more dangerous, and unfortunately, more frequent crimes involve rapists hiding in the backseat; predators posing as Good Samaritans; thieves waiting at stop lights; and carjackers who bump into you, then steal your car when you stop to check the damage. But you *can* protect yourself. Here are some useful tips to keep in mind:

1. Always lock your car when it's unattended—even for just a minute.
2. Check under your car and in your backseat before you get in.
3. Keep your purse and other valuables out of sight. If you must leave things in your parked car, cover them.
4. Don't risk running out of gas. Fill your tank as soon as you hit one-quarter full.
5. Drive with your doors locked.
6. Drive with your windows rolled up—all the way.
7. Don't stop in a deserted area or unsafe-looking neighborhood.
8. If you break down or are forced off the road, it is best to stay in your car. If you have an emergency CB or car phone, use it to call for help. If someone stops to help, do not open your door. Instead, lower the window just a crack, but not enough for them to get a hand in, and ask them to call the police. Do

not roll the window down or get out of the car. Check the identification of anyone claiming to be a police officer.

Protect Your Car from Theft

Car theft is cited as the number one property crime in America today. Every 26 seconds, a car is stolen in the United States. A skilled thief needs as little as ten seconds to steal a car, and most thieves require less than 60 seconds.

A recent listing of the ten most-often-stolen cars in California includes eight Japanese models. Their door locks and ignition devices seem to be less discriminating and enable thieves to file keys from similar cars to fit. Insurance statistics rate luxury and sports cars among the most desired targets for theft, particularly in urban areas.

Law enforcement officials emphatically agree that any theft-prevention device will probably be sufficient to deter most would-be thieves. Thieves simply prefer to hit an easier target.

Much like avoiding car crimes, keeping your car from getting stolen takes good common sense and a few guidelines. You can protect your car with these easy tips:

* Take your keys. Even if you're "just running in for a minute."
* Roll up your windows all the way.
* Lock your car. Always. Even inside your own garage.
* Park in well-lighted, attended garages or lots when possible.
* Keep packages, electronic equipment, and all valuables in the trunk.
* Place alarm stickers on the windows.
* Attach an inexpensive steering-wheel lock, available in auto parts stores for under $20.
* Replace golf-tee-shaped door locks with slim antitheft lock pulls.
* Install an alarm.

- Consider having an ignition or gasoline cutoff switch installed.
- Consider ignition locks, hood locks, or trunk locks.

Spend a few minutes with the salesperson at a good car parts store. Describe your parking habits and discuss the pros and cons of several options. Then install whatever you think you might need to get peace of mind.

What the Savvy Woman Keeps in Her Car

You can easily be prepared for almost anything you'll encounter out on the road. Having the right tools and resources with you can make the difference between taking control of an unwanted situation or becoming a victim. If you're stranded, your ability to fix the problem or call for help is essential. Take this list to a car parts store and find a helpful salesperson. Discuss your particular car and driving habits, as well as the pros and cons of each item. If you don't already know, ask how a particular feature works. Choose tools with features that suit your individual circumstances and needs. Make sure that you have these things on hand:

IN THE GLOVE COMPARTMENT OR OTHER HANDY SPOT:

AAA Card: Highly recommended for the savvy woman. Because it's smart to have a backup plan.

Emergency CB: Hand-held portable CB radio costs about $50 (much less than a car phone) and could save a life. Most good car parts stores carry them.

Owner's manual: A must for your glove compartment. Your dealer can get one for your car.

Tire gauge: Keep your tires inflated to the recommended pressure (which is printed on the side of the tire).

Flashlight: The kind with a red blinker may also serve as a road-emergency light at night. Be sure to check it often for working batteries or keep extras in the glove compartment.

Fire extinguisher: Keep the 2.75-pound dry chemical type secured under the front seat. Putting out a fire anywhere in your car may save your life.

Ice scraper: For that unexpected freeze while your car sits outside.

Fuses: One spare for each type your car needs. A service station mechanic can tell you which ones and how to change them (they're inexpensive and easy to install).

Rags/Tissues: For defogging the inside of the windshield or cleaning the dipstick when you check the oil.

Map: A must for your glove compartment.

Pen and paper: If you're in an accident, take the names of the individuals involved, their phone numbers, and insurance information. Take their driver's license number.

Quarters: For pay phones in case of an emergency. (As with any valuables in your car, keep them out of sight to avoid break-in temptation.)

Spare car key: In a magnetic key case in a very obscure location underneath your car or in your wallet.

Insurance card, registration, inspection certificates: These may be required by law in your state. If not, they will come in handy in case you're in an accident or pulled over by the authorities.

IN THE TRUNK:

Spare tire: Be sure your spare fits your car and is inflated. Check spare tire pressure two to three times a year.

Jack: You can change a tire quite simply. Support points for your car and jacking instructions are typically located inside the trunk or in your owner's manual.

Lug wrench: Used for removing the lug nuts on the wheel when you change the tire.

Hubcap locking wrench: To remove locking bolts on hubcaps so they can be removed. Check if your hubcaps have locking lugs to prevent theft.

Can of inflator/Sealant: If you can't change your flat, use this to inflate and temporarily seal low or flat tires with simple leaks.

Jumper cables: The twelve-foot length is better. Details on jump-starting your car are on page 26.

Empty gas can: Many gas stations won't lend you one. *Don't* carry gas in your car.

Funnel: Use it to fill your radiator, add oil or transmission fluid, or add gas from a can.

Siphon: If you can't get to a gas station, another driver may "lend" you a gallon or two.

Spare tools: Screwdrivers (conventional flathead and Phillips head), adjustable wrench, pliers, hammer, and pocket knife.

Duct tape: For temporarily sealing a leaking hose.

Safe Driving Tips

The ultimate safety device is the driver. Nothing in the world will protect you from harm as well as safe driving. It doesn't cost anything, there's nothing to install, and you can do it yourself. Here are some good guidelines to follow:

- Never drink alcohol before you drive.
- Drive only when you're well rested, especially on long trips.
- Adjust your seat so that you can comfortably reach the pedals, grip the steering wheel, and support your back.
- Adjust mirrors to enable you to glance without craning or straining.
- Familiarize yourself with all gauges and controls before driving an unfamiliar car.
- Check the gas and oil gauges before driving away.
- Wear your seat belt.
- Drive with your lights on. And remember to turn them off when you park—*all* of them. Even a map-reading light, if left on, can drain your battery completely.
- Keep your eyes on the road and concentrate on safety. Make caution your motto. Drive defensively. Be aware of other drivers' actions.
- Allow ample distance when following a car. Fifty yards is considered ample in most circumstances.
- Avoid aggressive drivers. Change lanes and let them pass.
- Stop and take a break periodically or when you begin to get weary, particularly on long trips. When and where you stop are important safety considerations. Avoid stopping in dark, desolate places. If you absolutely must stop in such a place, protect yourself by locking the doors and keeping your phone or CB handy. Most interstates have designated rest stop facilities in low population areas. Since they are usually well-lighted and used frequently by other travelers, you may feel safer. A good road atlas identifies mile markers and rest stops.

If You're in an Accident

We all hope we'll never have to deal with this. But savvy women know how to handle it just in case. Here's how:

1. IS ANYONE INJURED?

- If they are, don't move them
- Control profuse bleeding by applying direct pressure
- Keep the injured person warm
- Call for help and the police: phone 911 or CB channel 9

2. PROTECT ONCOMING TRAFFIC

- Put your emergency flashers on if they work
- Move cars if possible and if recommended by state officials. Some states prefer to leave cars until an officer completes an accident report.
- Have someone direct traffic

3. TURN OFF BOTH ENGINES

- Don't smoke! (If there's a gas leak, you may cause an explosion or fire.)

4. EXCHANGE INFORMATION

- Take the other car's license plate number
- Ask to see their driver's license
- Take their driver's license number
- Take correct, full name
- Take current address
- Ask for home and work phone numbers

- Ask to see their insurance card
- Take their insurance company name, phone number, and policy number
- Take the officer's name and badge number

5. GET WITNESSES

- Name, address, and phone numbers
- Discuss what they saw

6. DOCUMENT THE EVENTS

- Discuss what the other driver thinks
- Record a factual description of events
- Don't admit guilt
- Don't sign anything

7. CALL *YOUR* INSURANCE AGENT

How Important Is Performance to Your Safety?

The real question may be, "Is a high-performance car *safer* than other, less responsive cars?" The answer depends upon what's important to you. A car that is comfortable for *you* will be easier to control and will enable you to be a better driver. High performance vehicles are not necessarily safer. In fact, powerful super-charged performers may be more dangerous if you have less control. The same is true for cars that under-perform, are under-responsive, or have some malfunction. How can you judge that? Begin by answering these questions:

_____   Is the steering responsive to my command?

_____   Does it accelerate quickly and is there more power
              left if needed?

_____   Is the suspension solid with good "road feel"?

_____   Do I feel "in control" handling this vehicle?

_____   Do I feel comfortable while driving the car?

If you answered these questions with a "yes," then it probably
will be safer *for you.* Remember, all accidents are just that—
accidents. The car's performance was not designed to protect
you from an accident.

How Important Is Protection?

Head-on crashes cause about 50 percent of all car deaths and
serious injuries. But you can check how well your car will
respond to being in an accident. If you are in an accident, the
car's ability to protect you against the force of the crash may
keep you alive. It's that simple. Here's how to check:

1. The car's crash-test performance—your car's design, size,
   and weight determine how much of the impact the car ab-
   sorbs instead of you. U.S. Department of Transportation
   engineers measure how much of the crash force is absorbed
   by the occupant's head, chest, and thighs. Find comparative
   ratings in consumer reference books before buying your
   next car. Or look up the reports on the car you own. Bookstores carry a good selection of such resources in their automotive section.

   For information on the injury history and bumper performance of a particular vehicle, contact:

Highway Loss Data Institute
1005 North Glebe Road
Arlington, VA 22201

To verify the safety, defect, or recall history of a specific vehicle; to report vehicle defects; or to request copies of safety standards, equipment fact sheets, investigative reports, or consumer educational material, call:

National Highway Traffic Safety Administration
Auto Safety Hotline
(800) 424-9393 toll free
(202) 366-0123 in Washington, D.C.
(800) 424-9153 TTY for the hearing impaired
(202) 755-8919 in Washington, D.C., for the hearing impaired

2. Safety defects—every year, almost as many cars are recalled for safety-related defects as are sold. An astounding 170 million cars were recalled last year alone. Dealers can tell you immediately if your car has been recalled, for what, and when. The manufacturer must pay for it. If your car has been recalled, take it in now. And before you buy a new car, check its recall history.

3. Safety features to consider:

- Air bags
- Safety glass windshields
- Antilock brakes
- Childproof locks
- Head rest
- Safety belt tensioners
- Window/windshield visibility
- Centrally mounted rear window brake light
- Fuel tank located above or forward of the rear axle and located *within* the frame of the vehicle

A car salesman should be able to point out important safety features and explain how they work. Be sure to ask about the manufacturer's testing techniques and results.

A Word About Child Safety

Car accidents are one of the leading causes of death and serious injury for children. Since women usually have children in their cars more often than men, we need to understand how best to take care of them. The fact is that 80 percent of these accidents could be avoided by using seat belts and child safety seats. Children are not safe in the event of an accident if held only in your arms. The tremendous impact of an accident will literally rip the child away, possibly through the windshield. But you can make sure that your children are protected.

Many states' laws require child safety seats. Even if your state doesn't require them, use the best one available and use it every time a child rides in your car. Choose a safety seat that meets or exceeds federal motor vehicle safety standards. An official label will designate this compliance. Don't buy one without it.

Babies are best protected in a cradlelike infant restraint, which is secured facing the back of the vehicle. In the event of a crash, this position provides optimum protection to the head, neck, and torso. Children between four and seven years old need a booster seat to position them appropriately for the car's lap belt and shoulder harness. Without it, the seat belts are quite ineffective and could cause internal injuries due to improper placement in the event of an impact.

The center of the backseat is the safest place for your child's safety seat. This position offers the most protection on all sides in the event of an accident. Secure safety seats tightly and check them often.

You can take additional steps to minimize the risk of injury in the event of a collision. Give your child only soft toys or objects while riding. Avoid suckers, sticks, or hard objects that can cause choking or trauma. Put groceries and other heavy or loose objects in the trunk only. Injuries often result from the impact of flying objects inside the car.

Lock all doors. Be sure that your children don't play with knobs, buttons, handles, et cetera. Consider having child safety locks installed if you don't have them. And while you have children in the car, be a good role model by using your own seat belt every time you drive or ride. Children follow your actions in the car, just as they do everywhere else.

Winterize Your Car

Let's face it, the last thing you think about before the Thanksgiving holiday is having your car serviced. But that's exactly what you should think about first, before you find yourself stranded, because during the holidays, the roads are more hazardous with shopping mall congestion, drunk drivers, and freezing road conditions. Did you know that in extremely low temperatures, your car's battery loses half its strength? And an engine that needs tuning up is far more likely to break down in cold weather. If you have consistently followed the maintenance checklist in Chapter 5, these items should be in good shape. As winter approaches, you may want to take this checklist with you to ensure that your mechanic has double-checked these important safety measures.

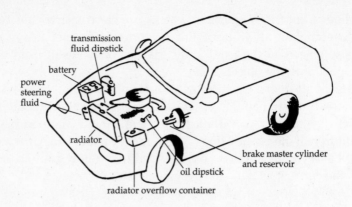

Figure 19. Fluid levels to be checked

To ensure optimum traction, stability, and control on ice and snow, check your car for:

_____	Adequate tire tread
_____	Proper inflation of tires
_____	Straight wheel alignment (steering doesn't pull to one side)
_____	Brakes are firm, not grabbing or loose
_____	Brake fluid is full

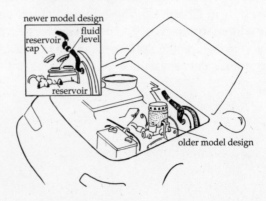

Figure 20. Reservoir for brake fluid

To ensure sufficient power to start your car in extremely cold temperatures:

_____ Battery fluid level is appropriate

Figure 21. Adding water to the battery

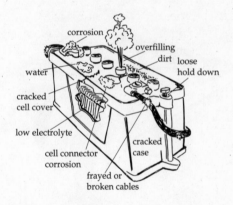

Figure 22. Checking the battery for wear

_____ Terminal connections to the battery are clean and secure
_____ Battery cables aren't worn or loose
_____ Spark plugs are all good and properly gapped
_____ Ignition system functions soundly

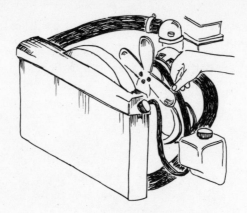

Figure 23. Checking fan belt tension

To protect your car's engine and operating ability in extremely cold temperatures:

_____ Fan belt not worn or loose

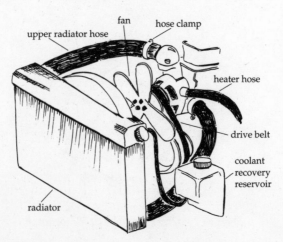

Figure 24. Hoses and belts

_____ Engine hoses strong and secure
_____ Antifreeze mixture is appropriate
_____ Oil is clean and full

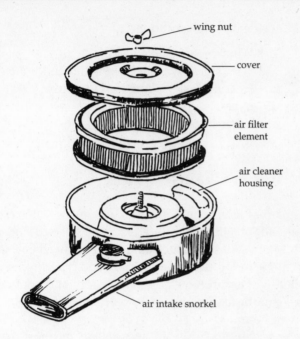

Figure 25. *Parts of an air filter*

Figure 26. *Using light to check the air filter*
_____ Air filter is clean

To optimize safe driving conditions:

_____	Windshield wipers work
_____	Windshield washer fluid is full and works
_____	Heating system functions properly
_____	Exhaust system functions properly, diverting exhaust to the outside

Snow Tires or Chains?

Tire chains may give you better traction and greater control over the road, but they're only effective if selected and used properly. Many states regulate standards for tire chains. Prices range from $30 to $60, depending on size and type. Professional installation will assure you of greater safety and confidence. Your mechanic or local garage should be able to install them in less than an hour.

Cross-link chains have biting edges and are the most conventional, but are more difficult to install.

Cable and plastic chains are lighter weight and sufficient for short-term use.

In some states, studded tires are allowed by law and may be a more attractive option. In less severe areas, all-season mud and snow tires have become popular and are designed for year-round use.

Discuss your options with family, friends, and your mechanic to decide what best meets your needs.

Foul-Weather Driving Tips

First, if weather is *really* bad, you may consider *not* driving when visibility is poor due to heavy snow, fog, or sleet, or if icy conditions have made the roads hazardous. If you feel uncomfortable or nervous about driving, or you are extremely tired, or even if you just don't feel up to it, then *do not drive*. You will be an accident waiting to happen. It's okay to call a friend, call a cab, or change your plans. Your safety is your most important consideration.

But, if you must make the trip, there are some savvy guidelines to follow to help get you there safely. You should always allow yourself extra time to reach your destination. Drive cautiously and defensively in foul weather. Avoid overtaking other cars and don't let another car force you to go faster than you want to. If a car is tailgating you, pull over to the side of the road slowly and let it go by. Try to keep your windows clear of ice and snow. Brush the snow from your hood, too, before you get into your car. Test your wipers to make sure they sweep freely, and clear the windshield before you put the car in gear. While driving in the evening and early morning, keep your headlights on. Remember to turn them off when you arrive. The last thing you want is a dead battery. Also, while driving, avoid sudden pressure on the brakes. This could cause you to spin and lose traction. Instead, pump your brakes easily and deliberately. If you have to go up a slippery hill, accelerate carefully and gain controlled momentum. Maintain steady pressure on the gas pedal to avoid losing traction.

Driving on Ice

Winter driving may be the most severe when a freezing cold front suddenly turns rain to snow and wet roads to ice. In addition to visibility concerns, this often occurs early in the season when drivers are likely to be inexperienced or unprepared. Anxiety rises, and the risk of accidents skyrockets.

Bridges and overpasses pose a bigger threat, since they freeze faster than solid ground and are often on an incline. Ice makes this combination a hazard to avoid whenever possible.

In any snow or ice condition, you can minimize skidding by accelerating and braking very carefully and deliberately. However, if you do skid, remember these tips:

- Don't panic.
- Take your foot off the accelerator.
- Gently pump your brakes.
- Steer *into* the direction of the skid until you regain control.

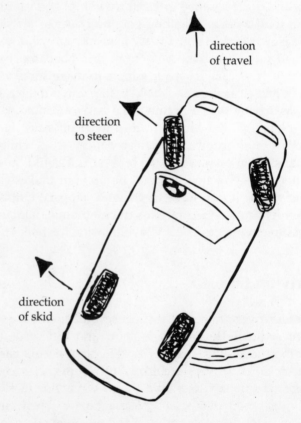

Figure 27. Steering into a skid

If You Get Stuck in the Snow

• Don't gun the engine or spin your tires. This will only make your traction problem worse by deepening the rut.
• Spread sand or gravel (or anything that will improve traction) in front of all tires that are spinning, particularly the rear tires. Your objective is to provide a foundation for your tires to grip.
• If you can't get out, call for help if you have a car phone or CB.
• If no phone or help is in sight, run your engine and heater about ten minutes each hour to stay warm.

In any event, avoid carbon monoxide poisoning by making sure your tail pipe is clear of snow and your exhaust escapes to the outside, not to the interior.

If You're Frozen Out of Your Car

Door locks may freeze when they're exposed to moisture and extremely cold temperatures. If your key won't work, try another door. It's possible that they're not all frozen. If that won't work, spray Deicer into it. If you don't have any at home, your AAA representative should be able to provide it. Or, your warm breath blown through a straw sometimes heats the lock enough to melt the lock components to insert a key. Heating your key with a match is not a smart idea, since the key could melt lock components or break off inside the lock.

When you can anticipate wet and icy conditions, particularly if your car must sit out overnight, place masking tape over the lock to keep moisture out.

PART II

A Healthy Car

4

How Your Car Works: Just the Facts, Ma'am

You can empower yourself in the world of cars without even knowing the first thing about car mechanics. To be savvy, you'll want to be familiar with this chapter before you speak with a mechanic about a suspected problem. Review the pertinent sections in this chapter to be sure that you have a basic understanding of the function and parts involved.

Essentially, all cars perform three fundamental tasks: creating power, using power, and controlling power. By understanding the basics of these general concepts, you'll be able to ask your mechanic questions that will help you evaluate the reasonableness of recommended repairs. This is vital to becoming a savvy car owner and is the single most important thing you can do to guard against unnecessary repairs. Your questions tell the mechanic that you are taking an informed, active role and intend to make thoughtful decisions (also see page 117 to Get It Fixed Right the First Time for a Fair Price). If the mechanic knows that you will question the necessity of each repair and insist on a detailed explanation that makes sense, you are much less likely to be persuaded to authorize unnecessary charges for parts and labor. When you have a basic under-

standing of the concepts, your questions will be on target. And
the mechanic will be alerted that you cannot be bulldozed. This
simple step acts as a major deterrent to rip-offs, just as a burglar
alarm sticker on your window helps to deter break-ins.

In each category, the basic information is presented in
question-and-answer format without being technical. If you'd
like to explore any of these areas more fully, many fine refer-
ences are available in bookstores and libraries for more detail.
(See the appendices for further reference.)

Creating the Power

1. How does a car move?

   The engine, transmission, and differential all work together
   to move the vehicle. The engine creates the power. The
   transmission and differential carry that power to the wheels
   to turn them.

2. How expensive are these to replace?

   The engine, transmission, and differential are the *most* expensive of all car parts to repair or replace. Sometimes these
   repairs may exceed the value of the car.

3. What parts might be involved?

   Major engine parts include:
   • Pistons
   • Connecting rods
   • Crankshaft
   • Flywheel
   • Camshaft
   • Valves
   • Cylinders
   • Ports
   • Torque converter
   • Heads

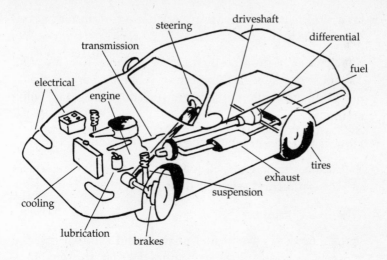

Figure 28. Car systems

4. How is fuel used?

First fuel has to be mixed with air. Then it goes into the engine's cylinders to produce power by converting the energy in gasoline into movement.

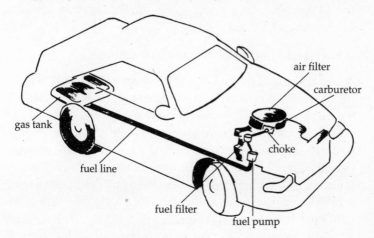

Figure 29. Fuel system

5. Why do I need to know if my car has a carburetor or fuel-injected system?

Repairs may be quite costly for these systems. You can avoid major expenses by catching minor problems early and asking your mechanic appropriate questions to avoid being scammed.

6. How can I find out which one it is?

Your owner's manual will tell you. Or, stop at a reputable service station and ask their mechanic.

7. What is a carburetor?

It regulates the air and fuel mixture and sends it into the engine's cylinders. Gas is pumped from the gas tank through a filter, then into the carburetor and on to the engine's cylinders.

8. What could go wrong?

There are 20 to 30 parts in a carburetor. If any are damaged, worn out, or need adjusting, your car won't run right. You may experience rough idling, rough acceleration, choking or flooding of the gas mixture.

9. What should I do to keep it running smoothly?

Avoid dirt roads if at all possible because dust and dirt clog filters. You should always try to keep your fuel filter clean. If it's dirty or clogged, your engine won't get enough gas and may surge and stop. Have your mechanic check and change it, if needed. Ask your mechanic if the fuel-and-air mixture is right. Too "lean" means too much air. Too "rich" means too much fuel. This may require adjustments in the choke, accelerating pump, power enrichment valve, or idling circuit. Keeping your air filter clean will also help keep your car running smoothly. Dirt inside your engine can be abrasive and cause expensive damage. Have this checked when you

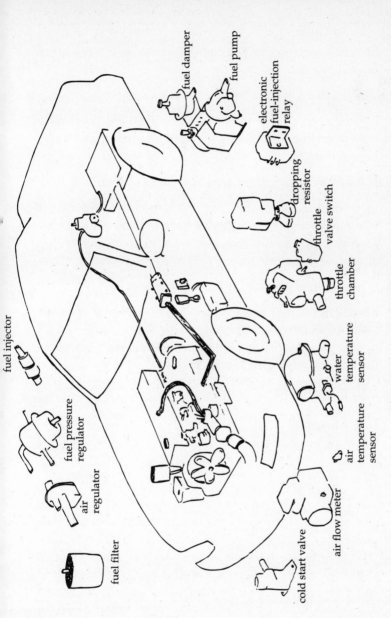

fuel injector

fuel pressure regulator

air regulator

fuel filter

fuel damper

fuel pump

electronic fuel-injection relay

dropping resistor

throttle valve switch

throttle chamber

water temperature sensor

air temperature sensor

cold start valve

air flow meter

Figure 30. Fuel-injection system

have the oil changed. (See page 65 on how to check your air filter.)

10. What is fuel injection?

It is the newer, electronic system that delivers fuel directly into the engine, eliminating the need for mixing fuel and air in a carburetor.

11. Is fuel injection better than a carburetor system?

It is much more reliable and less complicated than a carburetor system. It produces less exhaust and is more environmentally friendly. It is also more fuel efficient. In fact, almost all cars made since 1990 have fuel-injected systems.

12. What could go wrong with a fuel injector?

An electronic fuel injector (EFI) is electronically operated. Computer-controlled EFI systems are very reliable and seldom break down. However, if something does go wrong the repairs/adjustments may involve:

- Throttle chamber
- Computer
- Fuel injectors
- Electric gas pump
- Sock
- Fuel filter
- Manifold
- Throttle valve switch
- Airflow meter
- Throttle position sensor
- Fuel pressure regulator

13. What should I do to ensure its reliability?

Keep your fuel and air filters clean. Don't pump the gas pedal when you start your car. Pumping is not necessary with fuel injection.

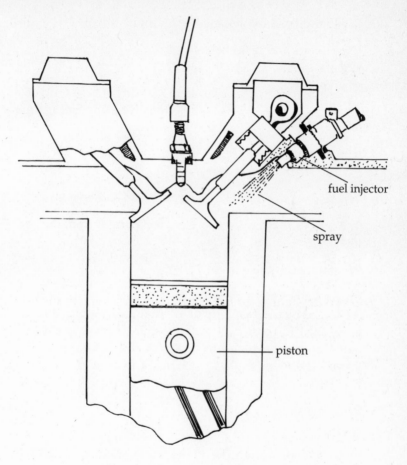

Figure 31. Fuel injector

14. How does the ignition system work?

The ignition system is responsible for igniting the fuel in the engine's cylinders. It converts 12 volts of electric current from the battery into 50,000 volts that energize the spark plugs and convert the energy in the gasoline into movement through thousands of controlled explosions within the cylinders.

15. What parts are involved in the ignition system?

- Cylinders and pistons
- Spark plugs
- Circuits
- Ignition coil
- Distributor
- Rotor
- Spark plug wires
- Crankshaft angle sensor

16. Where does the power come from?

The ignition system gets its electrical current from the battery.

17. What supplies the current?

Power comes from the battery. The battery is constantly recharged by the generator or alternator. (An alternator has been used in most cars in the last 20 years. It recharges better and faster than the generator did.) Other parts involved are belts, pulleys, electrical cables, and a voltage regulator.

18. What makes a car start?

When you turn on the ignition, two things happen: The battery sends current to an electric motor that spins the flywheel and rotates the pistons, drawing fuel into the cylinders. The second thing that happens is the battery sends a current to the spark plugs to ignite the fuel in the cylinders. When all this occurs simultaneously, the car starts. When it doesn't, the car either won't start or it won't run well.

19. Why does an engine overheat?

Fuel burns at 4,500° F, which is hot enough to burn metal. If it's not cooled, it will do major damage to your engine. The

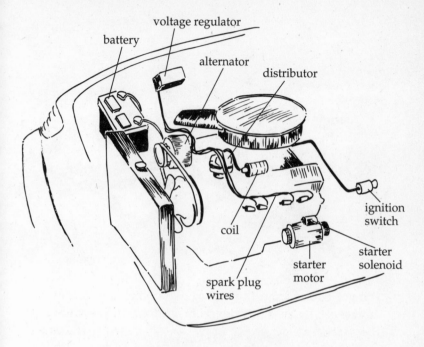

Figure 32. Electrical system

coolant (antifreeze and water) is circulated through the engine, where it picks up heat and carries it out of the engine. As it passes through the radiator, the coolant is cooled down before returning to the engine again to start the cycle over.

20. How can I avoid overheating?

Make sure you have the proper amount and mixture of coolant in your engine. (See page 31 for How to Check Your Radiator and Add Coolant.) If you have to fill your radiator regularly, it may have a leak. Have a mechanic check it. Make sure you have the proper thermostat to regulate the flow of coolant to the engine, and that it's working well. (See page 38 for what to do if your car overheats.)

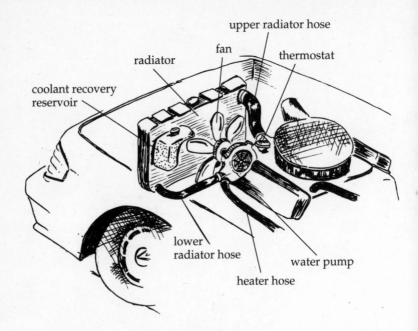

Figure 33. Cooling system

21. How does oil affect the engine?

Oil protects the engine's moving parts by easing friction. You must keep the oil pan full and clean to avoid excessive engine wear and a high repair cost to rebuild or replace an engine. (See page 29 for How to Check and Add Oil.)

22. How often should I change my oil?

Every three months or 3,000 miles is *highly* recommended. If you do, chances are you can avoid major problems and expenses. Changing the oil and the oil filter every 3,000 miles is the cheapest insurance you can buy. Check your owner's manual for grade recommendations to help you select a good quality of oil—never put used oil in your engine.

23. What does lubrication do for your car?

The lubrication system distributes and filters oil. Lubrication is essential to keep your engine running smoothly and keep engine friction to a minimum. The life of your engine is greatly enhanced and repair costs are minimized by keeping lubricants (including oil) clean and full. Parts involved include the pump, oil filter, and oil reservoir (crankcase).

24. How does a car cause pollution?

As fuel burns, residues—bearing gases—are produced. The exhaust system carries these spent residue-bearing

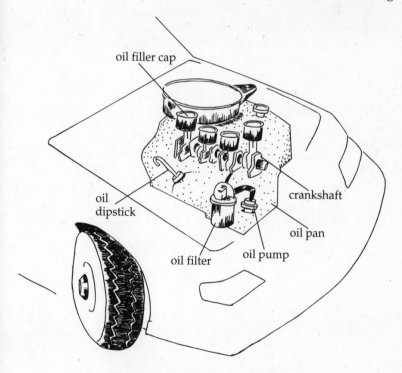

Figure 34. Lubrication system

gases out of the engine. The exhaust system consists of pipes and a muffler to carry these gases out of the engine and into the atmosphere. Emission controls are now mandatory and work to cut down on air pollution caused by car exhaust.

25. What are emission controls?

They consist of hardware on the exhaust system to recirculate and reburn these residue-bearing gases so that the final emissions to the atmosphere are cleaner and less harmful. Common emission controls include:

- Catalytic converter
- Exhaust gas recirculation system
- Crankcase ventilation system
- Fuel evaporation emissions control system
- Air injection reaction system

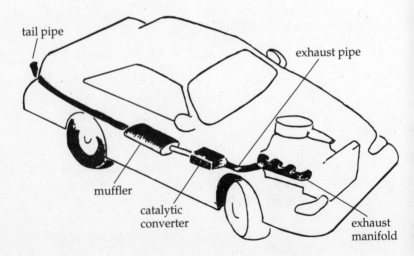

Figure 35. Exhaust system

Using the Power

1. How does power get to the wheels?

   The transmission and differential working together are called the power train or drive train. They transmit power from the engine to the wheels.

2. What is the difference between manual and automatic transmission?

   For the driver, the main difference is that a manual transmission has a clutch. You operate it with a foot pedal each time you shift gears.

3. What are the advantages of a manual transmission?

   It should last as long as the car lasts, with little or no maintenance. Transmission-related repairs may be significantly lower over the life of the car. Some people prefer the responsiveness of a manual transmission.

4. What are the disadvantages of a manual transmission?

   Clutching takes more effort, particularly in stop-and-go traffic. Clutches also wear out and need replacing, although this is much less expensive than replacing a transmission.

5. How can I avoid costly repairs?

   Automatic transmissions require a transmission oil and filter change every 25,000 miles, not just one or the other. Have your mechanic check this during your annual maintenance. (See page 98 for Quick Checklist and Maintenance Record.) If this isn't done, a clogged filter may prevent oil from getting through to the engine, which can then overheat and cause *major* damage.

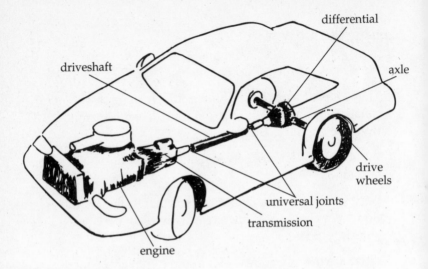

Figure 36. Transmission for rear-wheel drive

6. What is the differential?

Since your car must turn corners, the front and rear wheels closer to the turn travel a shorter distance than the outside wheels (on the other side of the car). The differential makes the outside wheels go faster so they keep up. If this didn't happen, the outside tires would drag and wear out.

7. What's front-wheel drive?

This system sends power to the car's *front* wheels to make it go. The differential is coupled to the transmission in the front of the car, rather than the rear. The transmission sends power to the front wheels via driveshafts, one to each side. The driveshafts are connected to the front drive wheels by flexible CV joints.

8. What do I need to know about front-wheel drive?

First of all, you can avoid costly repairs by keeping grease in the CV joints. Rubber "boots" cover and protect the CV joint

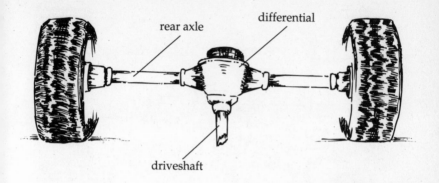

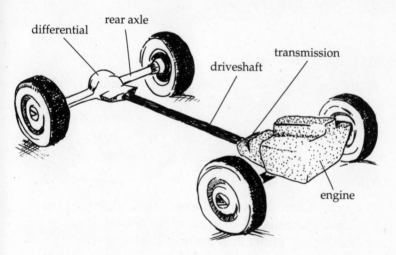

Figure 37. Driveshaft, differential, and axle for rear-wheel drive

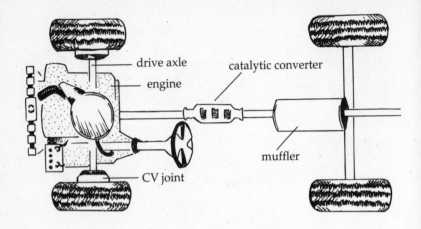

Figure 38. Front-wheel drive

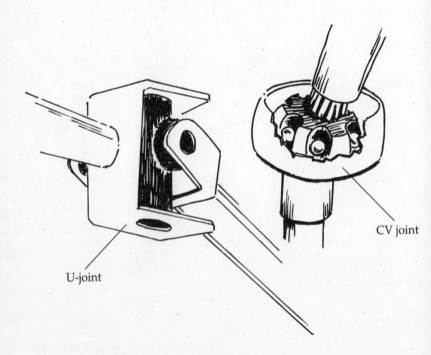

Figure 39.

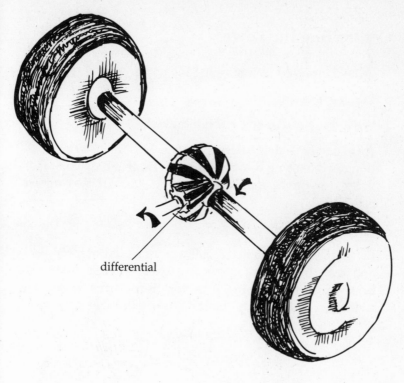

differential

Figure 40.

from water and dirt. Cracked or torn boots allow water and dirt in and that will cause early and expensive failure. Have both inspected and greased, if needed, when you have your oil changed, which should be every 3,000 miles (see maintenance checklist, Chapter 5.)

9. What if my car is not front-wheel drive?

If your car is rear-wheel drive, it has U-joints in the drive line. Have them checked for wear when you change oil, add lubrication, or if you hear humming or grinding while you drive.

Controlling the Power

1. What's involved in controlling the power?

   Braking, steering, and suspension system.

2. What do I need to know about brakes?

   A car can have disc or drum brakes. Most have a combination of both, using disc brakes in the front and drum brakes in the rear. Check your owner's manual to see how your car is equipped.

3. How do brakes stop the car?

   By using friction against a rotating surface. Front rotor discs and rear drums rotate with the wheel. A part inside the brake exerts force against the rotor disc or drum to stop the rotation, and thus, stop the car. For front disc brakes, these

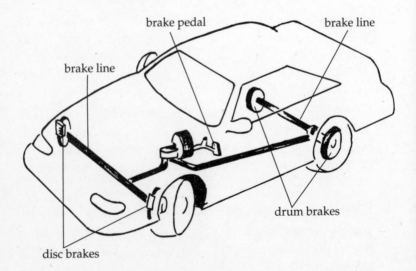

Figure 41. Brake system

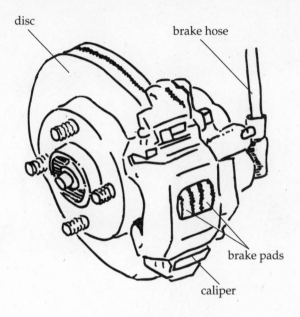

Figure 42. Disc brake (front)

parts are called pads. For rear drum brakes, they are called shoes or linings. When you step on the brake pedal, brake fluid contained in a reservoir in the master cylinder is forced outward and travels through tubing to each brake on each wheel. The brake fluid activates the pad or shoe to press against the disc or drum, causing friction and stopping rotation.

4. How can I avoid costly brake repairs?

Make sure you check your brake fluid if your brakes feel spongy or the pedal is low. Have your brake pads/linings checked every 12 months or 12,000 miles. Some brake pads and shoes are equipped with springlike clips that begin to rub on the rotor disc or drum when the pad or shoe nears the end of its life. If you hear a squeaking or scratching coming from a wheel when you step on the brake pedal, have a mechanic check it out soon, before the pad or shoe gouges a

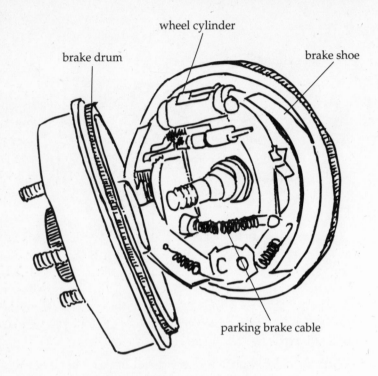

Figure 43. Drum brake (rear)

groove in the disc or drum, causing damage and a much
higher price for repair. Most will do a good visual brake
check free, and give you an estimate of cost.

5. What parts may be involved in brake repairs?

- Discs (rotors)
- Drums
- Pads
- Caliper
- Piston
- Semimetallic pads
- Master cylinder
- Plates

- Brake shoes
- Linings
- Wheel cylinder

6. What are antilock brakes?

   They are computer-coordinated brakes designed for an even stop. A computer detects when a wheel begins to turn at a speed that's different from the others. It adjusts the braking and speed of that wheel to be consistent with the others. It makes sure that all the wheels stop at the same time and with the same speed.

7. Why would I want antilock brakes?

   The best reason is that they're safer. If your wheels brake at different speeds, your car could easily go into a spin and you could lose control. However, as long as all four wheels slow the car at the same speed, the car will not spin. Antilock brakes are also good because they require no maintenance whatsoever. If any of their electronic parts fail, your brakes will still work, and you can still stop your car.

8. What should I know about steering?

   Most cars made after 1980 have rack-and-pinion steering for more dependable and responsive control.

   Parts involved include:

   - Rack (horizontal bar across the front of the car)
   - Tie rods
   - Steering arms
   - Front wheels
   - Pinion (gear on the end of the steering column)
   - Steering wheel
   - Steering column

9. What can go wrong with power steering?

   You may lose power steering fluid due to a leak. Have it checked monthly. (See page 98 for Quick Checklist and Maintenance Record.) The power steering fluid should not

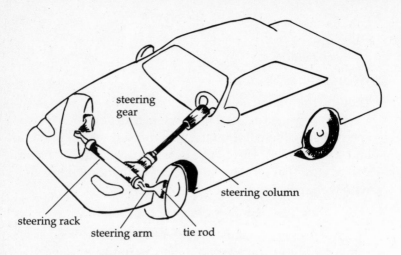

Figure 44. Rack-and-pinion steering

evaporate or be used up. If it's disappearing, have a mechanic check for a leaky hose or pump. Another precaution
is to have the power steering pump drive belt checked
yearly for wear.

10. What is the suspension system?

The car's springs, shock absorbers, and tires work together
to provide a safe and comfortable ride.

11. What's important to know about the suspension system?

Shock absorbers (shocks) eventually need to be replaced,
usually indicated by excessive bouncing. They can be replaced without removing the springs. Springs should out-
live most cars.

   Tires can last 50,000 miles or more if you keep them
properly inflated (see page 22 for How to Check Tire Pressure and Add Air). You should keep your tires properly
balanced and rotated and keep the car's front end aligned
properly (see page 98 for Quick Checklist and Maintenance
Record).

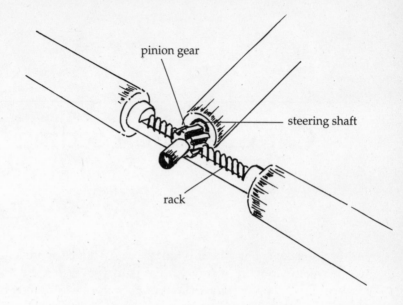

Figure 45. Rack-and-pinion steering: detail

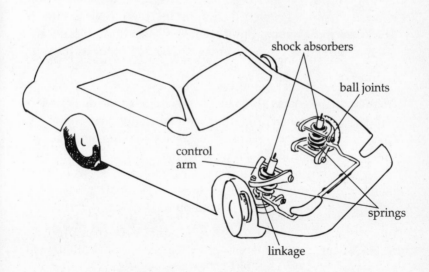

Figure 46. Suspension system

5

Car Care and Feeding

"Have you taken your vitamins today? . . . An ounce of prevention is worth a pound of cure. . . . Eat your vegetables. . . . An apple a day keeps the doctor away. . . . Starve a cold, feed a fever." These bits of wisdom have survived many generations because they help. They keep us healthy and help us to avoid getting run down and becoming susceptible to sickness. Of course, when we get sick, it's important to go to the doctor to find out what's wrong. But if we take the age-old precautions, we may not go as often or it may not be as serious as it could have otherwise been.

What does it cost when your car doesn't get its vegetables (regular maintenance)? Chances are, the cost is lower when regular maintenance precautions are taken and symptoms are treated early. Whatever a repair costs, it usually seems like too much, and it's probably an unwelcome surprise. This chapter gives you the information you need to schedule preventive maintenance, judge the reasonableness of repair prices, and anticipate a few of the more common repairs. Using this information as a guide will help you stay in charge and control your car costs.

What Difference Does Regular Maintenance Make?

Consumer Reports recently surveyed over 8,000 automobile owners who had driven their cars over 100,000 miles. One-fourth of those surveyed had exceeded 140,000 miles. Seventy-eight percent of the cars were over ten years old. The results were that more than one-third hadn't experienced any mechanical problems in the year prior to the survey. Only 1 percent said their cars were nearing the end. Seventy-five percent of the cars were domestic. The survey asked key questions, including, "What is most important to the longevity of your car?" The answers:

Action	*Percent Responding*
Regular maintenance	74 percent
Careful driving habits	20 percent
Fix problems immediately	13 percent
Keep car clean and garaged	11 percent
Use quality replacement parts	5 percent
Find a good mechanic	5 percent
Do-it-yourself maintenance	4 percent

Your car can last a long, long time if you take care of it. And, by following the regular maintenance schedule, your car will take care of you by delivering you safely to your destination and helping you avoid costly repairs.

Use the following maintenance checklist every month. You'll find that it's easy to use and universally understood. By following it closely, you'll protect your investment and keep it running like a dream.

Quick Checklist and Maintenance Record

MONTH 1: _____ Year: _____

Engine Mileage: _____

	Date Completed	*Cost*	*Serviced By*
CHECK FLUIDS:			
Engine oil	_____	_____	_____
Coolant	_____	_____	_____
Automatic transmission or hydraulic clutch	_____	_____	_____
Power steering	_____	_____	_____
Brake	_____	_____	_____
Battery	_____	_____	_____
CHECK TIRE PRESSURE:	_____	_____	_____
COMMENTS:	_____		
	_____		
	_____		
	_____		

MONTH 2: _____ Year: _____

Engine Mileage: _____

	Date Completed	Cost	Serviced By

CHECK FLUIDS:

Engine oil _____ _____ _____

Coolant _____ _____ _____

Automatic
transmission
or hydraulic
clutch _____ _____ _____

Power steering _____ _____ _____

Brake _____ _____ _____

Battery _____ _____ _____

**CHECK TIRE
PRESSURE:** _____ _____ _____

COMMENTS: _____

_____

_____

_____

MONTH 3: _____ Year: _____

Engine Mileage: _____

	Date Completed	_Cost_	_Serviced By_
CHANGE:			
Oil	_____	_____	_____
Oil filter	_____	_____	_____
CHECK LUBRICANTS:			
Manual transmission	_____	_____	_____
U-joints	_____	_____	_____
Rear end	_____	_____	_____
INSPECT CV JOINT BOOTS:	_____	_____	_____
CHECK FLUIDS:			
Coolant	_____	_____	_____
Automatic transmission or hydraulic clutch	_____	_____	_____
Power steering	_____	_____	_____
Brake	_____	_____	_____
Battery	_____	_____	_____
CHECK TIRE PRESSURE AND SPARE:	_____	_____	_____
COMMENTS:	_____		
	_____		

MONTH 4: _____ Year: _____

Engine Mileage: _____

	Date Completed	*Cost*	*Serviced By*

CHECK FLUIDS:

Engine oil _____ _____ _____

Coolant _____ _____ _____

Automatic
transmission
or hydraulic
clutch _____ _____ _____

Power steering _____ _____ _____

Brake _____ _____ _____

Battery _____ _____ _____

**CHECK TIRE
PRESSURE:** _____ _____ _____

COMMENTS: _____

_____

_____

_____

MONTH 5: _____ Year: _____

Engine Mileage: _____

	Date Completed	Cost	Serviced By

CHECK FLUIDS:

Engine oil _____ _____ _____

Coolant _____ _____ _____

Automatic
transmission
or hydraulic
clutch _____ _____ _____

Power steering _____ _____ _____

Brake _____ _____ _____

Battery _____ _____ _____

CHECK TIRE PRESSURE: _____ _____ _____

COMMENTS: _____

_____

_____

_____

MONTH 6: _____ Year: _____

Engine Mileage: _____

	Date Completed	Cost	Serviced By
INSPECT FUEL SYSTEM AIR FILTER:	_____	_____	_____
ADJUST MECHANICAL CLUTCH:	_____	_____	_____
CHANGE:			
Oil	_____	_____	_____
Oil filter	_____	_____	_____
CHECK LUBRICANTS:			
Manual transmission	_____	_____	_____
U-joints	_____	_____	_____
Rear end	_____	_____	_____

	Date Completed	*Cost*	*Serviced By*
INSPECT CV JOINT BOOTS:	_____	_____	_____
CHECK FLUIDS:			
Coolant	_____	_____	_____
Automatic transmission or hydraulic clutch	_____	_____	_____
Power steering	_____	_____	_____
Brake	_____	_____	_____
Battery	_____	_____	_____
CHECK TIRE PRESSURE AND SPARE:	_____	_____	_____
COMMENTS:	_____		
	_____		
	_____		
	_____		

MONTH 7: _____ Year: _____

Engine Mileage: _____

	Date Completed	*Cost*	*Serviced By*
CHECK FLUIDS:			
Engine oil	_____	_____	_____
Coolant	_____	_____	_____
Automatic transmission or hydraulic clutch	_____	_____	_____
Power steering	_____	_____	_____
Brake	_____	_____	_____
Battery	_____	_____	_____
CHECK TIRE PRESSURE:	_____	_____	_____

COMMENTS: _____

_____

_____

_____

MONTH 8: _____ Year: _____

Engine Mileage: _____

	Date Completed	Cost	Serviced By
CHECK FLUIDS:			
Engine oil	_____	_____	_____
Coolant	_____	_____	_____
Automatic transmission or hydraulic clutch	_____	_____	_____
Power steering	_____	_____	_____
Brake	_____	_____	_____
Battery	_____	_____	_____
CHECK TIRE PRESSURE:	_____	_____	_____

COMMENTS: _____

_____

_____

_____

MONTH 9: _____ Year: _____

Engine Mileage: _____

	Date Completed	Cost	Serviced By

CHANGE:

Oil _____ _____ _____

Oil filter _____ _____ _____

CHECK LUBRICANTS:

Manual
transmission _____ _____ _____

U-joints _____ _____ _____

Rear end _____ _____ _____

**INSPECT CV
JOINT BOOTS:** _____ _____ _____

CHECK FLUIDS:

Coolant _____ _____ _____

Automatic
transmission
or hydraulic
clutch _____ _____ _____

Power steering _____ _____ _____

Brake _____ _____ _____

Battery _____ _____ _____

**CHECK TIRE
PRESSURE AND
SPARE:** _____ _____ _____

COMMENTS: _____

_____

MONTH 10: _____ Year: _____

Engine Mileage: _____

	Date Completed	Cost	Serviced By
CHECK FLUIDS:			
Engine oil	_____	_____	_____
Coolant	_____	_____	_____
Automatic transmission or hydraulic clutch	_____	_____	_____
Power steering	_____	_____	_____
Brake	_____	_____	_____
Battery	_____	_____	_____
CHECK TIRE PRESSURE:	_____	_____	_____
COMMENTS:	_____	_____	_____
	_____	_____	_____
	_____	_____	_____
	_____	_____	_____

MONTH 11: _____ Year: _____

Engine Mileage: _____

	Date Completed	Cost	Serviced By

CHECK FLUIDS:

Engine oil _____ _____ _____

Coolant _____ _____ _____

Automatic
transmission
or hydraulic
clutch _____ _____ _____

Power steering _____ _____ _____

Brake _____ _____ _____

Battery _____ _____ _____

**CHECK TIRE
PRESSURE** _____ _____ _____

COMMENTS: _____

_____

_____

_____

MONTH 12: _____ Year: _____

Engine Mileage: _____

	Date Completed	Cost	Serviced By
CHANGE AUTOMATIC TRANSMISSION FLUID OR HYDRAULIC CLUTCH FLUID:	_____	_____	_____
FLUSH COOLING SYSTEM AND INSPECT HOSES:	_____	_____	_____
CHECK BELTS:	_____	_____	_____
CHECK BRAKES:	_____	_____	_____
INSPECT BATTERY:	_____	_____	_____
INSPECT EXHAUST SYSTEM:	_____	_____	_____
CHECK POWER STEERING FLUID:	_____	_____	_____
ROTATE TIRES:	_____	_____	_____
BALANCE TIRES:	_____	_____	_____
CHANGE:			
Oil	_____	_____	_____
Oil filter	_____	_____	_____

	Date Completed	*Cost*	*Serviced By*
CHECK LUBRICANTS:			
Manual transmission	_____	_____	_____
U-joints	_____	_____	_____
Rear end	_____	_____	_____
INSPECT CV JOINT BOOTS:	_____	_____	_____
INSPECT FUEL SYSTEM AIR FILTER:	_____	_____	_____
ADJUST MECHANICAL CLUTCH:	_____	_____	_____
COMMENTS:	_____
	_____
	_____
	_____

What Repairs Will Cost You

Each car and every repair job is unique, with its own circumstances and complications. Price varies drastically, depending on the make, model, year, and condition of your car, as well as local fluctuations in costs of components, labor hours required, and the extent of damage and repairs. Also, because women are seen as targets for car repair scams, they get charged higher rates. An average labor hour charge is typically $45, which also varies by location, mechanics' expertise, and competitors' current promotional pricing. However, you can be savvy to the "ballpark" range of costs for repairs in common categories.

Use this guide to give you a basis for judging the reasonableness of a repair shop's price quote. But be sure to get a second or third opinion from other repair shops and ask trusted family and friends for their experience. Ultimately, you must decide what's reasonable to you.

Component	Price Range
ENGINE AND TRANSMISSION	
Distributor assembly	$200–500
Electronic-control computer	$150–1,200
Electronic-ignition module	$125–300
Emission system check	$35
Engine analysis	$35 and up
Engine, compression test	$35–55
Engine, minor tune-up	$80–125
Engine belt (one)	$45–55
Ignition coil	$65–125
Oil pan	$200–350
Oil pressure sensor	$30–125
Oil pump	$200–500
Timing belt/chain	$160–300
Transmission overhaul	$400–625
Valves, adjust (all)	$75–600
Valve lifters (all)	$250–400

Component	Price Range
FUEL AND EXHAUST	
Catalytic converter	$35–45*
Exhaust manifold	$200–350
Fuel filter	$40–50
Fuel gauge, tank	$100–210
Fuel injection, clean system	$35–40
Fuel injection, check	$65–75
Fuel injector (one)	$110–225
Fuel pump	$175–325
Fuel pump, pressure test	$25–35
Fuel tank	$225–325
Muffler and pipes	$85–175
PCV valve	$20–30
ELECTRICAL	
Alternator	$175–475
Battery, test	$15
Battery, replace	$25–85
Battery cables (all)	$100–200
Charging system, check	$30
Ignition switch	$30–150
Starter	$175–325
Voltage regulator	$100–500
COOLING	
Cooling system, check	$20
Cooling system, clean/flush	$65–150
Radiator	$60–110
Radiator hose (2)	$65–110
Thermostat	$40–55
Water pump	$150–250
Water temperature sensor	$30–60
BRAKES, STEERING, AND SUSPENSION	
Alignment, check	$25–30
Alignment, front	$45–85
Alignment, rear	$35–65
Axle shafts, front (2)	$200–850
Bearings, front (2)	$125–425

Component	Price Range
Bearings, rear (2)	$125–475
Brake job, complete	$225–300
Brake cylinder, master	$200–300
Brakes, adjust	$10–20
Brakes, bleed	$10
Brakes, inspect	$30–35
Calipers, front (2)	$275–800
Control arms, lower (2)	$145–380
Drums, rear (2)	$145–200
Parking brake, adjust	$10–20
Power steering hose	$50–325
Power steering pump	$300–550
Shock absorbers/strut, rear (2)	$100–375
Shock absorbers/strut, front (2)	$135–375
Steering gear	$425–1,150
Tie rod (one)	$85–175
Wheels/tires, rotate	$30

ACCESSORIES

Air-conditioning, check	$50
Air-conditioning, charge	$100
Air-conditioning compressor	$350–650
Blower motor	$75–300
Headlamp	$30–150
Heater core	$120–280*
Heater hose	$30–65*
Power-window motor, front	$100–250
Washer pump	$25–60*
Wiper arm and pivot (each)	$70–135
Wiper motor	$125–300

* Labor only—does not include parts cost.

Your Aging Auto

Even when you diligently care for your car, check the fluids, and keep up on maintenance, you should expect to repair or replace certain parts along the way. The question is, what's a reasonable lifespan for car parts? The Automotive Parts and Accessories Association, an industry trade group, has compiled the following list to help you judge:

Component	Expected Life (MILES OR YEARS)
ENGINE AND TRANSMISSION	
Electronic-control (computer) unit	80–100,000
Electronic-ignition module	100,000
Engine belts	40–60,000
Oil pump	Lifetime
Timing belt	60–100,000
Timing chain	100,000
Valve lifters	Lifetime
FUEL AND EXHAUST	
Catalytic converter	100,000
Fuel filter	30–40,000
Fuel injector	100,000
Fuel pump	70–90,000
Fuel tank	Lifetime
Muffler and pipes	50–80,000
PCV valve	30–40,000
ELECTRICAL	
Alternator	80–100,000
Battery and cables	three to five years
Starter	80–100,000
Voltage regulator	80–100,000
COOLING	
Radiator	100,000
Radiator hoses	40–60,000
Thermostat	40–60,000
Water pump	70–90,000
BRAKES, STEERING, AND SUSPENSION	
Automatic transmission	Lifetime
Clutch	40–60,000

Component	*Expected Life* (MILES OR YEARS)
Control arm, lower (ball joint)	70–90,000
Disc-brake pads	30–40,000
Disc-brake calipers	70–90,000
Drum-brake shoes	30–40,000
Drum-brake cylinders	70–90,000
Front-axle shaft	70–90,000
Power-steering pump	80–100,000
Shock absorbers	25–35,000
Springs	70–90,000
Struts	40–60,000
Tie rod	70–90,000
Universal/CV joint	70–90,000

ACCESSORIES

Air-conditioning compressor	80–100,000
Heater core	70–90,000
Horn	100,000
Power-window motor	60–90,000
Washer pump	70–90,000
Wiper blades	20,000/one year
Wiper motor	70–90,000

6

Get It Fixed Right the First Time for a Fair Price

For years it seemed to me that car mechanics and repair shops operated by some closely guarded grand plan that we women would never be privy to and that certainly would never become public knowledge. I thought that repair shops must have a secret code to communicate among themselves and conjure up their elaborate schemes for ripping their women customers off. After all, it always seems they've "got us" one way or another because we didn't know anything about cars.

Well, it's just not so. Yes, scams certainly do exist. You can fall into them unknowingly and lose a lot of money. In fact, the key is that you are much more likely to fall into them *unknowingly*. That's exactly what I did when I became the unsuspecting target of a transmission scam.

My car's automatic transmission was slipping. I could tell something was wrong because it made an unusual whirring sound when it shifted gears. At the same time, the tachometer needle was jumping higher than it ever had before. And it just didn't feel right when it shifted into third gear. So, I took it in for a diagnosis. My favorite trusted mechanic confirmed that it needed transmission work. After all, it was four years old and had 80,000 miles on it. That really wasn't unreasonable. The only problem was that he didn't work on transmissions.

My first mistake was not following through with the mechanic he suggested I use. I am quite certain that his recommendation would have alleviated a lot of heartache for me. It's a good bet that when someone you trust through experience gives you a reference on someone they trust, you're likely to be satisfied, too. This turned out to be a $2,000 lesson.

My next mistake was deciding to use a certain transmission shop primarily based upon best price. Never, never allow this to be the most important criteria in your choice. My transmission repair was initially quoted at $350. Great news, I thought. But this quote turned out to be part of the scam. When they got my car into their shop, pulled the transmission apart (once they do that, you are dependent on them), they informed me that it was a bigger job than they had anticipated and it would cost $2,000. Of course, they offered to put it back together for the original $350 so that I could have it towed elsewhere for a second opinion. But they couldn't put it together until next week. I was furious!

By this time, I had already spent a week hassling with the transmission problem, interrupting my work, and paying for a rental car. The prospect of extending this fiasco for a couple more weeks would be more costly for me in terms of time and money. This was clearly a lose/lose situation. I negotiated an additional six-month comprehensive warranty and authorized the full repair with an unconditional price ceiling. Even with these concessions, I felt disappointed, foolish, and, above all, angry.

After another week, the shop called to inform me that my car was ready. I paid the bill and tried to be positive about the whole thing.

But the frustration didn't end there. To my absolute astonishment, the transmission slipped several times on the way home!

Could it be that they didn't do the repair at all? Did they do an unnecessary transmission repair? Or did they just do incompetent work? I had no way of knowing myself, so I took the car back. They agreed to keep it, drive it, and figure out the problem. After another week, they denied that it had a problem. They claimed that it didn't slip when they drove it. We went back and forth for the next two years. The transmission never worked right again.

The lessons I learned through this experience and others like it are here to benefit you without your having to pay drastic prices. You can avoid a lot of despair by taking a little time up front, exploring your options, carefully considering the alternatives, and thoughtfully implementing your decisions. You *can* take charge and arm yourself against these injustices.

Competent, reliable, trustworthy repair shops *do* exist. But finding them and being in charge does not happen by accident. By following the basic steps in these following pages, you'll demystify the process, become independent, and shed the victim role. There's truly no secret scheme or Grand Plan to intimidate and take advantage of us women that we cannot combat. And we can make sure that we don't allow it anymore.

Finding the Right Shop for Your Repair Work

You may need more than one shop for different types of service. Each one has unique advantages and disadvantages. Consider them carefully before you commit yourself to their service. There are lots of choices. In choosing one for your needs, consider the following:

- What repair is necessary?
- What are you willing to pay?
- Are they friendly/helpful/service-oriented?

- What are your instincts about their integrity?
- What are your friends' recommendations and experience with the shop?
- Is the staff courteous, qualified, and efficient?
- Is the staff properly identified?
- Are facilities clean, safe, and comfortable?
- Is the garage clean and orderly?
- Do they keep sufficient insurance?
- Do employees get periodic training?

You may choose different shops for specialized repairs. Generally, your choices are dealers, department stores, specialty shops, service stations, or private auto repair garages. Here are some tips to help you decide which one is best for the repairs you need:

Dealers
Such as Ford, Honda, Buick, et Cetera

Advantages	*Disadvantages*
Repairs under warranty may be free	Repairs past warranty may be more expensive than other repair shops
Newer cars will be serviced by specially trained mechanics for that exact vehicle	You usually don't get to talk with the mechanic. A service representative takes your repair order and passes it on to the mechanic. Inadequate or inaccurate information may result in delays or incomplete repairs
They may be motivated to do a good job to entice you to buy your next car there	You may not be allowed inside the service garage itself to evaluate the facility
They have the right tools, training, *and* right test equipment	You may have to leave the car all day (or several days) until they get to it. Not much personal service

Department Stores' Auto Repair Departments Such as K mart, Montgomery Ward, et Cetera

Advantages	Disadvantages
May be less expensive	You may not get to talk to the mechanic who works on your car
Usually open longer hours, even on weekends	The advertised specials may be their way to get you in, analyze your car for other maintenance and repairs, then sell you on them
May be conveniently located; you can shop or do errands while you wait	Mechanics are probably less skilled in specific cars and their idiosyncracies than at a dealer
Mechanics with good *general* training	
They often run advertised specials on regular maintenance work	Probably have less test equipment for newer high-tech cars and problems

Specialty Shops
Such as Firestone Tire and Auto, Midas Muffler, Express Lube, et Cetera

Advantages	Disadvantages
May offer special deals and lower prices	You may not get to meet the mechanic who works on your car
They may have a mechanic who is certified in the specialty	They also may try to get you to buy other maintenance and repairs
Their location and hours are usually convenient	

Service Stations
Such as Exxon, Mobil, Texaco, Local Gas Stations with Service Bays or Service Centers

Advantages	Disadvantages
May offer lower prices	Mechanics may be more general and less specialized. It may take longer to diagnose and repair a complicated problem
May be close to your home	They may employ only one mechanic, so you're relying on only one person's expertise
If you get your gas there, you can develop a relationship of service and trust	

Private Auto Repair Garages
Usually Locally and/or Privately Owned

Advantages	Disadvantages
You can usually get to know the owner and/or mechanic	Very high-quality private auto repair shops are hard to find
You can often find a shop that specializes in your make car	
Prices may be lower than the dealer	
The owner may be much more concerned with his reputation, so you may get better service	

How to Find a Good Mechanic You Can Trust

Don't wait until you need repairs and are in a bind. A few hours spent now may save you hundreds of dollars, many hours of wasted time, and unnecessary frustration.

1. Ask your friends, relatives, and co-workers who they trust and who they *don't* trust.
2. Before you use a mechanic, call the Better Business Bureau. Ask if any complaints have been filed against the shop.
3. Ask to see their mechanic's certification. Certificates are usually hung on the walls, or patches worn on the mechanic's uniform. The National Institute of Automotive Service Excellence (ASE) is the industry standard for competence. Mechanics can be certified in up to eight areas:

   • Engine repair
   • Automatic transmission/transaxle
   • Manual drive train and axles
   • Suspension and steering

- Brakes
- Electrical systems
- Heating and air-conditioning
- Engine performance

4. Look for AAA approval. Since 1975, AAA-approved shops must meet these minimum standards:

   The shop must offer an ASE-certified mechanic or equivalent for each service offered.

   They must offer a minimum of services, including: engine tune-up, minor engine repair, brake and electrical services, and either suspension and steering or heating and air conditioning. Always check to make sure the work is overseen by a *qualified* supervisor.

   Service representatives are trained to advise customers about services. Their reputation may be checked through researching:

   - Financial reports on the shop
   - The Better Business Bureau
   - Past customer surveys

5. It's smart to test the shop's service and work with a small repair or maintenance job. If you're satisfied, try them for more complicated work.

What to Do Before You Leave Your Car at the Shop

Armed with the appropriate information, you will be in charge when you take your car in for a diagnosis. Before you go, use this simple list to make sure you've covered the important points:

1. Get a basic understanding of how your car works, particularly the systems you suspect may need repair. (See Chapter 4.)
2. Fully describe the car's symptoms. (Refer to Chapter 2 to double-check your list.)

   What sounds funny? When?

   What smells funny? When?

   How does it act funny? When?

   Does it happen consistently? Or when? Be specific.

3. Make an appointment when you can allow plenty of time to discuss it. Bring this list and discuss it with the mechanic to ensure that each point is thoroughly covered. Take the mechanic for a drive to demonstrate the problem, if necessary.

As the customer, your needs must be heard and understood. If you feel that they aren't listening or aren't responsive to you because you are a woman you may be in the wrong shop. Service attendants and mechanics will treat you with respect if you insist upon it through your actions. These are the key points to remember as you present your problem and begin to evaluate the service you receive:

1. Describe your car's symptoms only. Don't tell them what you think it needs. If it doesn't need that, you may get and pay for it anyway.
2. Don't act helpless. Be assertive and don't be intimidated.
3. Ask what the mechanic suspects the problem may be. Beware of general statements. Ask them to be specific.
4. Ask them to explain *in detail* what needs to be repaired, why, and what it will cost. Ask how many labor hours will be required. Ask friends and co-workers if this sounds reasonable. Do your research.

5. Ask for their labor rate. It may range from $25 to $50 per hour or more.
6. Be aware of how they treat you:

   • Do they listen attentively?
   • Do they appear to care what you want?
   • Do they treat you with respect?
   • Do they take the time *you need* to understand the repairs?
   • Do they answer your questions graciously, giving you answers that make sense to you?
   • Do they give you the time you need to make *your own* decision, with no pressure?

7. If it is a large repair, you may want to get a second opinion.
8. Don't necessarily go for the lowest price. This may be a scam to get your business, then the garage may "up" the price later "due to complications." (Remember my transmission scam story in the introduction to this chapter.)
9. Don't authorize repairs until you are satisfied that it's reasonable and fair. Don't let them pressure you. Remember: You are the customer.
10. Get a written estimate.
11. Don't sign a blank work approval form. Sign only for specified repairs you agree to.
12. Stipulate on the work order a maximum dollar amount you are authorizing. Instruct them *in writing* on the work order (just above your signature) that repairs exceeding a specific dollar amount must be authorized by you *before* they are performed, or you will not pay for them.
13. Be sure to ask if the work is warranted and get it *in writing*. Ask: "Will this fix the problem completely?"
14. Ask them to save the old parts. You may want to stipulate this on the work order.

What to Do Before You Pay for Your Repairs

Before you pay, test drive your car. A few minutes now could save you money, time, and frustration. Once you've paid and driven away, it's much more difficult to prove that your repair wasn't right. After you test drive, ask the mechanic to give you the old parts and explain the problem as well as the repair. Thoroughly examine the repair bill. Ask questions to your heart's content if you don't understand something. You must make sure the warranty is on the bill. If it's not, get it in writing. Keep all your repair, maintenance, and service records and receipts in one place. Let the manager or owner know what you think of the service you received. They will remember your praise and treat you well the next time. If you were dissatisfied, speak up! Present the specific reasons, along with why you feel you weren't treated right.

Beware of These Typical Scams

Recent independent studies concluded that in the United States, correct diagnosis and repair of an automotive problem occurred only 28 percent of the time! In order to avoid rip-offs and scams, you must take charge of the situation. Taking charge starts with performing all scheduled and preventive maintenance using the checklists in Chapter 5. Then trust your senses to detect any symptoms of malfunction. Does anything sound or feel strange? Does anything look or smell unusual? Again, if your instincts tell you that your car is acting up, it probably is.

Familiarizing yourself with the basic concepts presented in Chapter 4 will give you the foundation of information and awareness you need to ask meaningful questions. Scams and charges for overpriced or unnecessary repairs typically happen to individuals who ask few questions and are less involved in the decision-making process. Let your mechanic know that you intend to ask questions and get the information verified, perhaps even get the opinion of another mechanic, before you authorize repairs. This should not be a problem if they have your best interests in mind. If this upsets your mechanic, watch out. You may want to find a more customer service oriented shop.

You can avoid scams and pricing schemes before you become a victim. A few of the most common scams are not elaborate or tricky. You can quickly detect them if you are aware of what to watch for and probe when you suspect foul play. Here are a few things to watch for:

Scam	*Solution*
Repair shops may advertise astonishingly low prices for certain repairs, then try to sell you on more lucrative (and perhaps unnecessary) repairs to make up their profit.	Be wary of such low-ball pricing offers, particularly if they try to convince you that this additional work must be done before they can complete the work you've authorized.
Shops may be so bold as to charge you for repairs that were never made. A typical example of this is the deceptive operator who charges you for a new alternator when only an inexpensive alternator belt is needed.	Always ask to see the old parts the mechanic has removed from your car and the new parts that he will install in your vehicle. Insist on this before you pay and stand there as long as you must to see the parts, even if it means they must put your car back up on the hydraulic lift.
Many service shops charge "flat rates" for standard repairs, even though the mechanic can perform the repair in much less time (up to half).	Ask the service manager what their repair policy is. Better shops will charge only for the mechanic's actual time if it's lower than the flat rate.

Scam	Solution
Travelers, particularly the elderly, are more susceptible to roadside service station scammers when they stop to fill the gas tank while going to a distant place. Your license plates will signal that you don't live nearby, and a short conversation with you may confirm that. These scammers are betting that since you live far away, you will not pursue them even if you suspect deception. Examples include such dishonest practices as selling you a new tire after deliberately puncturing one of yours, or squirting oil on your engine to simulate a leak or other engine problem.	You can be friendly without giving this stranger any information about yourself. Watch the attendant very carefully as your car is being serviced. Do not leave your car unattended to go inside or to the rest room until your service has been delivered and paid for. If you suspect deception, call the local police right away.
Tune-ups or repairs are performed and you are charged for them, even though they should be covered under your warranty.	Check your warranty before authorizing any work on your car. Dealers are obligated to perform this work *free*, regardless of where you bought your car. Be extremely vocal. Take your grievance to the manufacturer's regional office or corporate headquarters if necessary.
You've paid for repairs shortly after your warranty expires. They would have been covered under your now expired warranty.	Have a pre-expiration warranty inspection performed. Take your warranty and have the mechanic inspect all covered items. Get a written report of his findings. Request immediate repairs, if needed, in writing from the dealer.

Scam	*Solution*
You are charged for a full brake job when an inexpensive replacement of pads or linings would have been sufficient.	Have your brakes checked regularly, according to the maintenance checklist on pages 98 to 111. Early detection of wear will help you avoid unnecessary work. If you suspect a scam, get a second or third opinion.
You pay for major transmission repairs your car did not need.	The presence of some small metal particles in the oil pan does not necessarily mean you need a major overhaul. Check with the Better Business Bureau and get a second or third opinion.
You overpay for a complete tune-up when a simple, periodic maintenance tune-up would do.	On many cars built after 1981, a label in the engine compartment indicates the need for tune-up. Check your owner's manual. Many cars need only a spark plug, fuel filter, and air filter replacement every 30,000 miles or so. Labor charges for this should generally not exceed 30 minutes. If your car still isn't up to par after a proper tune-up, ask for a diagnosis of the engine management systems.

Scam	Solution
You pay for fuel-injector cleaning by your mechanic.	Rough idle, engine misfire, and poor gas mileage *may* be the result of clogged fuel injectors due to bad gasoline. Use several tanks of a good-grade fuel to flush the injectors clean. Special gasoline additives can also clean the injectors while you drive.
You are sold wheel alignments that you don't need.	If your steering wheel shimmies above 40 mph, a wheel balancing may be all you need to correct the problem. Insist on doing only that first. Then test drive your car. If it pulls hard to one side, you may also need an alignment.
You are sold new struts or shocks to fix steering vibration.	New struts or shocks almost never solve steering vibration problems. You can tell if your car needs new ones, though. Lean on each side of the bumper and bounce the car a few times, then release it. If the car continues to bounce more than once, you probably do need them. Repeat for each corner.
Your cooling system is not properly flushed.	Before the work is performed, ask your mechanic to drain the engine block and *back flush* the entire system.

Scam	Solution
Air-conditioning is recharged and serviced improperly.	If a mechanic simply adds more R-12 refrigerant, it may work, but much less effectively. The proper procedure entails *evacuating* the system with a special vacuum pump. Insist on this.

Use a Credit Card for Repair Fraud Protection

If you feel your repairs were incorrectly or incompletely performed, you may have an effective negotiating tool if you paid by credit card. By federal law, you have the right to withhold payment for the amount in dispute. In order to qualify, the repairs must exceed $50 and be made in your home state (or within 100 miles of your home). You must first try to work out the problem with the mechanic. Document these efforts by sending letters or making detailed notes of your discussions, including dates and all representations made.

If the problem is not resolved through your efforts, send a certified, return-receipt letter to the credit card company and a copy to the repair shop. Explain the problem and request a specific resolution or settlement. The credit card company cannot collect interest or penalties on the amount in dispute. However, if your credit record is affected, you have the right to have your story reflected in your file.

If you have additional questions about your rights, contact:

Federal Trade Commission
Credit Practices Division
601 Pennsylvania Avenue NW
Washington, D.C. 20580

PART III

Savvy Savings

7

Slash Your Car Costs in Half (or More)

Did you know that:

- An automobile is the second largest investment for most people?
- The average price of a new car is well above $16,000?
- Most people buy about 15 cars in their life and spend $225,000?
- If you finance your cars, that amount will increase to $325,000?
- You can cut your automobile costs in half (or more) by buying durable cars and driving each one to 150,000 miles?
- You can achieve this by following just a few simple steps?

Think of it: $12,548 was the median annual income of single females in 1990, while $16,012 was the average new car price. New car prices have risen 111 percent since 1980 and 352 percent since 1970! Cutting your car expenditures in half could yield a significant sum of money annually to save, invest, or spend as you wish.

The Strategy That Works

Most people keep each car only three years and drive it only 50,000 miles. If you extend the life of your car, you will cut your cost by *more* than half! It involves a little-known strategy that the car industry prefers to keep secret. Automobile manufacturers and suppliers would be severely affected if we cut our new car buying by two-thirds. New car sales in America represent over 74 percent of all car purchases and generate $96.6 billion in sales annually. Cutting consumer spending by two-thirds would devastate their profit structure and change their business forever. So it's up to us to be savvy in our car-buying decisions.

By using the following strategy, we're pocketing profits, instead of letting the car industry benefit at our expense. In the first three years, a new car depreciates about 50 percent in value. Most of this depreciation occurs in the first 18 months. So if you, like most Americans, replace your car after three years, you will repeat this cycle of heavy loss due to devaluation. Every three years you will lose at least 50 percent of the value of your car. You may continue to owe more on the car than it's worth, thereby never building equity. However, if you *keep* your car, depreciation slows to only 30 percent during the next three years. This 20 percent savings begins to add thousands of dollars to your discretionary spending. After six years, your vehicle will average only 3 percent depreciation annually. Now your savings are easily exceeding five digits. When properly and consistently maintained over its life, a durable car will last 150,000 to 200,000 miles. (See Chapter 5 for Car Care and Feeding.) As you pay the note, depreciation slows down considerably after three years and your car begins to hold its market value. At this point, the market value of your car begins to exceed the loan balance. The cost of regular maintenance and repairs due to normal wear and tear shouldn't deplete the savings you've achieved. By driving your car to

150,000 miles, you avoid repeated, heavy losses due to depreciation and build equity in your car. This ultimately saves you over $100,000 during your lifetime.

Easy, Inexpensive Things to Do to Save Money

The single most important thing you can do is to change your oil and filter consistently every 3,000 miles, and be sure to *keep* your oil level at or near full. (Ten-minute lube and oil-change facilities are great.) Be sure to:

- Review your owner's manual and follow the maintenance schedule closely.
- Change all other fluids and filters regularly as prescribed.
- Watch your indicator gauges and lights. Be aware of changes in your car's performance. Take care of small problems right away. They never take care of themselves. Spend money on preventive maintenance before it snowballs.
- Have periodic tune-ups and keep all your service records in a file in one place.
- Keep a log of your gas mileage.
- Minimize the number of times you start your car when it's cold. A cold start puts approximately the same wear on your car as 500 miles of driving it warm.
- Avoid driving on dusty roads. (Dust clogs filters and bearings and cuts the engine's life.)
- Don't rest your foot on the brake or clutch while you drive, and avoid stop-and-go driving.
- Avoid idling for extended periods.
- Minimize heavy loads or pulling trailers.
- Use a gas with a fuel-system cleaner in it.

Treat your car right and it will treat *you* right.

It's Easy to Figure Your Gas Mileage

Your gas mileage can help you monitor car costs. Not only will you be more conscious of unnecessary driving by watching your fuel consumption, but it may also alert you to potential problems. Excessive fuel consumption may be an indication of a mechanical problem. A small notebook in your glove compartment is handy for tracking it, and once you start, it can be interesting to watch for trends.

			Example
1. Fill the tank and record your miles:	_____	A	8,537
2. Drive until you need another fill-up.			
3. Fill the tank and record your miles:	_____	B	8,823
Record the number of gallons you purchased:	_____	C	12.6
4. Calculate B−A=D: This is the number of miles you traveled on this tank of gas.	_____	D	286
5. Calculate D÷C=E: This is your miles per gallon (mpg).	_____	E	22.7

Fast Facts and Techniques to Save Gas

You'll probably spend $1,100 a year on gas, assuming you drive 15,000 miles, get 15 mpg, and pay $1.10 per gallon.

Here's how to save money:

- Most cars get the best gas mileage at about 45 mph. Driving 70 mph (as opposed to 55 mph) costs you one-third more in gas, or up to $365 a year.
- Driving with the windows open can cost you up to 10 percent more in gas (due to wind resistance and drag).
- Short trips eat up gas. A two-mile trip with many stops can get as little as 10 percent of your normal gas mileage. You'll save 50 percent of your $1,100 annual gas bill ($550) if you drive only highway or freeway miles. You'll also improve your gas mileage by driving after your engine warms up, so consolidate your errands.
- An idling engine uses about a gallon of gas each 90 minutes. You'll save gas if you turn the engine off, rather than let it idle for 60 seconds or more.
- Brake only when necessary. Don't drive with one foot resting on the brake. Most drivers brake about 50 percent more than needed. Brake less by staying farther back in traffic and driving at a steady pace.
- A standard transmission may save you as much as 5 percent in gasoline costs. It gets the best gas mileage in the higher gears. At 20 mph, you can save 20 percent by shifting to third gear.
- In a car with standard transmission, keep your foot off the clutch pedal.
- You can save $3 or more each time you fill up by using the exact octane that your car needs. (Don't buy $1.70 premium if your car runs perfectly well on the $1.40 variety.)
- You'll get better fuel economy and avoid clogged fuel injectors by using gasoline with: high detergent content, fuel-system cleaner/conditioner, and a deposit-control additive.
- It's easy to lose a half gallon of gas by overfilling your tank. Instead, place the gas nozzle deep into your tank and stop when the pump clicks off. Don't squeeze more in. When the pump clicks off, you can get that last half cup of gas that's in

the hose by simply lifting the hose higher than the handle while it's still in your tank.

- A locking gas cap could save you the cost of replacing at least one tank of gas siphoned by thieves, or gas that spills out while driving.
- A fuel-injected engine is usually more fuel efficient.
- A 10 percent smaller engine can save you 6 percent in fuel.
- You can save $70 a year in fuel costs by adding a can of MoS_2 (molybdenum disulfide) each time you change the oil. (Get it at an auto parts store.)
- An oil labeled "Energy Conserving II" improves gas mileage up to 3 percent. That's like getting a free half gallon of gas with each fill-up.
- Save up to 10 percent in gas by driving on radial tires. After 40,000 miles, this could leave you with $300 more in your pocket. The narrower your tires' tread, the better the mileage, so avoid extrawide tires.
- Keeping your tires inflated properly can save you $100 a year in better fuel economy (not to mention $50 a year in tire wear).
- Four-wheel drive vehicles use more gas than two-wheel drive vehicles.
- Rear-wheel drive vehicles use more gas than front-wheel drive vehicles.
- Most of the gas-saving devices on the market offer only limited hope for savings and sometimes don't really work at all.
- Carpooling ten miles to work each way can save you $500 a year in gas.
- Get a copy of the most recent EPA gas mileage guide if you're considering buying a new car. Call the National Highway Traffic Safety Administration's hotline number: (800) 424-9393.

8

What You Need to Know About Insurance

Why Buy Insurance?

A split-second accident could cause you personal financial disaster without the appropriate amount and type of insurance. For instance, if you were uninsured or underinsured and at fault in an accident that left a physician unable to practice medicine ever again, the judgment against you could force you to declare personal bankruptcy. But even that would not relieve you of the responsibility of paying the judgment, a sum that could devastate you financially for the rest of your life. Every vehicle you own, including boats, motorcycles, snowmobiles, should be properly insured. Check the Declarations section of your policy to ensure that each vehicle is listed separately.

Who is typically covered in automobile policies?

- You
- Your spouse, if living in the same household

- Family members who are children and living in the same household, if you give them permission to drive the vehicle
- Read the declarations section carefully to make sure you know specifically who is covered
- If you carpool, be sure to examine a copy of each driver's car policy to ensure that medical coverages are adequate for all passengers, not just family members or occasional passengers
- If you rent a car, your policy may or may not cover you for collision damage and rental car liability. Examine your personal car policy as well as the rental car company's rental agreement before deciding whether or not to accept additional insurance when you rent a car. Low deductible limits and high liability coverage will give you more protection

Shop for Savings

You can save a lot of money by aggressively comparison shopping for the best rates. Call several different insurance agents and ask for quotes from each. Rates vary by as much as 100 percent among insurance companies. It is important to find an agent who is knowledgeable and willing to spend time with you. Find a good agent you have confidence in and whose judgment and advice you trust. Get recommendations from your friends, family, and co-workers. AAA members can take advantage of a free insurance counseling and advisory service. If you have a lot of questions and need to learn more in order to make cost-effective decisions, this is an excellent resource. But, as with any commission-based insurance counselor, be sure to make purchase commitments only after careful consideration.

Rates vary drastically with the type of vehicle, in relation to expected repair costs, history of theft rates, vehicle performance (including speed), and body construction/protection. Rates also vary depending on types of coverage you desire, amounts of coverage, amounts of deductibles, your driver classification, and your geographic residence.

First, to be sure that an insurance company is stable, ask your agent about the rating of the company. During the 1980s, many insurance companies experienced severe loss, fraud, and failure. Use only the largest companies with the best rating. Individual states are the primary regulators of insurance companies. But they have no jurisdiction over how insurance businesses are run. The State Insurance Commissioner's office collects financial information about each insurer such as their annual convention statements and Schedule M. You can request this information directly by phone. All insurance companies are rated, usually by A. M. Best. They provide information on insurers' financial condition, brief history, management, operating commitments, and geographic area. A. M. Best's ratings are a compilation of strengths and weaknesses in four areas: Underwriting (new business), Expense control, Reserve adequacy (expected claims), and Investments.

In general, place your insurance only with companies rated A or A+ by A. M. Best. You can find Best's ratings in your local library, or by writing to:

A. M. Best Company
Ambest Road
Oldewick, NJ 08858
(908) 439-2200

Three other major firms also rate insurers, and their ratings are usually stricter. You'll want to call them yourself, or check your local library. Rating systems differ, so simply comparing ratings is not meaningful. Choose insurers that consistently rate high among all rating systems.

Moody's (212) 553-0377
Standard & Poor's (212) 208-1527
Duff & Phelps (312) 368-3157

Or, get the special ratings issue for $10 from: The Insurance Forum, Box 245, Ellettsville, IN 47429.

The toughest measure of all is published by a firm that evaluates whether or not a company could survive a severe recession. The information costs $15 by phone: Weiss Research (800) 289-9222.

The Six Basic Types of Insurance

Type	Coverage
Property damage liability	If you damage others' property, this pays for their repairs and your legal defense. Most states require you to carry at least $10,000 per person and $20,000 per accident. However, your actual coverage should be $50,000 per accident or greater, due to the high cost of cars and the potential for damage to multiple cars.
Bodily injury liability	If you injure or kill a pedestrian, or passengers in other vehicles or your own, this pays for your legal defense and any damages assessed against you. You should carry an amount that equals or exceeds your net assets plus potential legal fees.
Medical payments	If injuries result, regardless of fault, this pays for medical expenses. $1,000 per person is the standard policy coverage. But by paying a small additional premium, you may raise this amount to provide benefits that cover the deductible and coinsurance payable for most health insurance policies.

Type	Coverage
Uninsured motorist	If you are injured by an uninsured or hit-and-run driver, this pays damages to you and any injured passengers. It is imperative because an astounding number of drivers do not have insurance. In the Chicago area, half the drivers on the road are uninsured. A reasonable amount of coverage provides $100,000 per person and $300,000 per accident.
Collision	If your car is damaged in an accident, this pays for repairs to your auto regardless of fault. Collision deductibles and premiums have an inverse relationship. Consider the trade-off between lower deductibles and higher premiums. Compare alternatives to find the most cost-effective combination for you.
Comprehensive	If your car is damaged from fire, theft, vandalism, natural disasters, et cetera, this pays for repairs to your car. Comprehensive coverage deductibles directly affect premiums similarly to collision deductibles. Look for a policy that provides benefits sufficient to repair or replace the damaged or lost property.

Have your agent explain these in more detail. What risks seem most threatening to you? How much would you be able to pay out of your pocket in the event of a claim? What premiums are you able to pay? Think of some good "what-if" situations and questions for your agent to answer before you decide what coverage to buy.

Your state may have specific requirements. Ask your agent to explain them to you.

Manage Your Insurability

In recent years, insurance rates have skyrocketed and consumers feel cheated. We're paying more for less insurance. Even worse, most insurance companies are searching for ways to drop high-risk clients. The fact is, if you've had a ticket or an accident, you're classified as a high risk.

Smart policyholders protect their insurability by raising their automobile deductibles to $500 or $1,000 and filing claims only for catastrophic losses. The higher deductibles will lower your premium by as much as 30 percent to 60 percent. Don't file claims under $500. If you do, the insurer will be likely to raise your premiums by as much as 25 percent, or drop you entirely. And once you've been dropped by an insurance company, most insurers classify you as uninsurable and decline your application for coverage altogether at any price.

Tips to Reduce Your Premiums

1. Be sure to comparison shop. Ask the agent if they offer any special discounts.
2. Increasing your deductible from $250 to $500 could reduce your annual premium by 15 percent to 30 percent.
3. Drive an inexpensive used car that can be insured for the minimum.
4. You may opt to decline collision and comprehensive coverage if your vehicle is worth less than $2,000.
5. Some companies offer discounts for:

   - Low-mileage driving
   - Nonsmokers
   - Nondrinkers

6. Insuring more than one vehicle in your household on the same policy can save you 15 percent to 20 percent.

7. Companies may also offer discounts for:

   - Drivers over the age of 50 or 55
   - Ride-share commuters
   - Economy cars
   - Lower-cylinder engines
   - Cars with airbags
   - Antitheft devices
   - Antilock brakes
   - Defensive driving courses
   - Students with high grade averages
   - Sole female drivers between 30 and 49 years of age
   - Good drivers (no moving violations for three years)
   - Having a homeowner's policy with the same company
   - Farm use

8. Your insurance company may match a quote given on identical coverage by a competitor.
9. Think twice about the high-cost relative benefit of extra coverages such as towing, car rental, and audio equipment. They are generally quite expensive for very low benefit.
10. Before you choose an insurer ask your agent how much your premium will increase after a ticket or accident. Consider this when making your purchase decision.

You can call the Insurance Information Hotline at (800) 221-4954 toll free, from 9:00 A.M. to 4:45 P.M. (EST) for answers to your insurance questions.

Insurance Claims for Accident or Loss

After an accident, we're usually so agitated that it's tough to think clearly. To help you sort things out and deal with the aftermath, follow these guidelines:

1. Notify the police in the event of any violation of law, such as hit-and-run or uninsured motorist.

2. Notify your insurance agent as soon as possible. Your agent will be able to explain detailed procedures for your situation and provide the necessary forms to submit. Do this immediately.
3. If police are involved, obtain copies of all their reports.
4. Cooperate fully with the insurer's investigation.
5. Send the insurer copies of pertinent legal notices, reports, or papers you receive.
6. If you feel that the investigation or handling of your case is not appropriate or fair, you may wish to seek the advice of an objective attorney. A brief initial assessment of your case should not cost you anything. Ask about this up front, preferably before you make an appointment.

PART IV

Car Buying and Selling

9

Buying Your Car
(Yes, Yourself)

Arm Yourself: Information Is Power

After opening my own car dealership, I've learned that the car business is really not as mysterious as it seemed as a consumer. You can quickly learn what you need to know to get a fair deal, and still allow the dealer to make a reasonable profit to keep their company alive. We rely on this win-win philosophy and our customers appreciate it.

Whether you buy your car new, or shop for a dependable used car, some of the secrets of the trade are important to understand from the dealers' perspective in order to get the best deal. Many times customers pay excessive profits when they could have negotiated a lower price or a more favorable package. Or they are so concerned about the amount of their monthly payment that they end up negotiating a package that is much costlier in the long run. By understanding what motivates the dealer and taking the time necessary to gather key information, you will save thousands of dollars on each purchase.

Every car transaction is unique. Each one has its own combination of circumstances that affect the negotiation and price. They include:

- The car you are considering
- Your flexibility in your choice
- How much time you have to shop
- Time of year you are buying
- Time of month you are buying
- Market conditions
- Dealer inventory
- Your financial situation and credit history
- How much the salesperson knows about your needs
- How good the salesperson is

Negotiations and pricing also greatly depend upon your financing method and disposition of your current car. Generally, your deal will fall into one of these categories:

- You intend to finance a new or used car; with or without a trade-in.
- You intend to pay cash for a new or used car; with or without a trade-in.

Thorough preparation is the single most important thing you can do to get the best price during negotiation. Setting specific objectives up front along with a good knowledge of the negotiation process will put you in control of creating a win/win outcome. You do this by defining your desired outcome, as well as understanding dealers and their motivations for a minimum "win" or profit.

Let's start with understanding the dealer. Who's involved?

The Salesman: Salesmen are trained to ask questions, understand customers, and convince them to buy *today*. They average eight to ten sales a month, making up to $200 in commission per car. Each sale is important to them. As you interact with the salesman, you must ask yourself, "Do I really want what he is suggesting, or am I being manipulated?"

The Sales Manager: When price negotiations begin to stall, the salesman will bring in his manager. The sales manager's job is to close the sale at a price that is more favorable to the dealer. They are pros at persuasion. Don't cave in. Stick to your offer. Walk away when they don't agree. (They'll generally call you in a few hours to get you to come back.)

The Business Manager: Their job is to increase the dealer's profit by selling you high-profit-margin add-ons and extended warranties after you have negotiated the deal. Add-ons may include credit life insurance, disability insurance, rust proofing, paint sealant, fabric guard, and alarm systems, among others. Add-ons and extended warranties are customarily overpriced. Resist the temptation to buy them.

Car salesmen are some of the toughest, tightest negotiators around. Their job depends on getting the most money for each and every car they sell. This often results in a win/lose situation—they win and we lose.

Your job is to get the salesman to accept a win/win situation. You can do this with no formal training in cars or negotiating. Simply prepare yourself with the techniques in this chapter and practice your negotiating style before you shop seriously.

Car dealerships will ultimately agree to sell you the car you want for $200 to $500 over their invoice. Be prepared to negotiate with them *extensively* before they will accept this minimum profit. But remember throughout your negotiation that they *will* usually settle for "a bird in the hand" ($200 profit) today, over the unknown higher profit they might get sometime later. Persistence and savvy handling of the salesman is the key. If one particular dealer lets you walk away, another dealer *will* do your deal.

How to Decide Which Car Is Really Right for You

Before you shop for a vehicle, determining what you are looking for and its market value is the most important thing you can do. These two things *must* be done *before* you talk with salespeople.

To determine what kind of car you are looking for, before you set foot on a car lot, make a list of your needs. Things you might consider include:

- How much can you afford to spend?
- How many passengers will you carry?
- Do you need a station wagon? Hatchback?
- How many doors?
- Do you haul things?
- Do you pull a trailer?
- Will you use it for business? Sport?
- Do you drive in adverse conditions? On hills?
- What safety features are important?
- Do you prefer automatic or manual transmission?
- What power features are important (door locks, windows, steering, brakes)?
- Is air-conditioning a must?
- What gas mileage do you need?
- How long do you intend to keep the car?
- How important is projected resale price to your decision?

Now that you've defined your needs, decide on several cars that meet them. It's time to do a bit of easy research:

1. Find the *Consumer Reports* comparison of new or used cars in your local library or bookstore, or obtain "AAA Autotest" from AAA for unbiased evaluations of test results on over 125 imported and domestic models.

2. Determine the pros and cons of each model you've picked.
   Compare:

   - Safety
   - Handling and performance
   - Reliability
   - Comfort and luxury
   - Economy
   - Usefulness

3. Choose one or two specific models and identify all options
   and features you must have. Write these down in detail.

Now determine the car's market value:

1. Keep in mind:

   - For new cars, the dealer's sticker price is too high. It has a
     lot of built-in profit.
   - For used cars, the condition and mileage will affect its
     value.

2. Consult any of the following sources to determine market
   value, including all features and options you have chosen.

   - *NADA Official Used Car Guide*
   - *Kelley Blue Book*
   - *Edmund's New Car Prices*
   - *Edmund's Used Car Prices*

3. Never pay retail. Buy only at wholesale or below. When
   buying a car, it is *imperative* that you know the dealer's cost.
   Refer to Edmund's or other price guides for current dealer
   cost information. Armed with this information, you can determine the price that provides the dealer with a *minimum*
   "win" profit, about $200.
4. Know the value of your trade-in. Consult the same sources
   and write this down. Sell for only wholesale or above. Your

vehicle's mileage will greatly impact the value and mar-
ketability of your used car. Total mileage that exceeds an
average of 20,000 miles per year is considered high, and will
decrease the value of your car. Conversely, total mileage
averaging less than 10,000 miles per year is generally considered low, and may increase the value of your car. The used
car valuation guidebooks contain mileage tables for adjusting stated market values. These tables are always used to
decrease values for high mileage.
5. Find out what the prime rate is and what reasonable financing rates are for used cars.

Should You Buy New? Used? or Lease?

What's right for you? Here's a quick comparison to help you
determine which option works best.

NEW CARS:

Advantages	Disadvantages
Unlimited selection of color, interior, and options	New vehicles usually depreciate 50 percent in the first three years
Reliable and covered under warranty	Higher price
Condition and value is easily determined	
Dealers may provide financing and rates may be lower	
You can keep a history of the vehicle's service and repairs	

USED CARS:

Advantages	*Disadvantages*
Lower price and/or lower monthly payments	Condition and value must be carefully assessed
Previous owners usually take the most depreciation	Reliability may be questionable
	Limited selection of color, interior, and options
	Warranties are usually not available
	Service records are usually not available
	Financing is usually up to you to arrange and rates may be higher

LEASING:

Advantages	*Disadvantages*
Usually less cash required	Stricter credit requirements
Monthly payments may be lower	Insurance costs are usually higher
Lease cars (usually new) are reliable and covered under warranty	Early termination usually carries penalties
Lease terms may be flexible	High mileage usually carries penalties
Lease cars may have tax benefits (if used in business)	A lease usually doesn't build equity
	Lease provisions may be deceptive

Advantages	Disadvantages
	It is usually costly to change the terms of your contract midlease
	At the end of the term, the car's condition may cause serious (legal) disputes

What Exactly Is Leasing?

Leasing is an enforceable legal contract to pay some amount of money over a specified period of time for the right to use the automobile. You have no ownership rights to the vehicle and will not build equity. All terms of a lease may be negotiated. Your success in negotiating the terms you desire are completely up to you. There are typically two types of leases: open-end and closed-end.

With an open-end lease, you bear the risk that at the end of the lease term the car is not worth the estimated residual value you agreed to in the contract, which could be as unrealistically high as 45 percent of the price of the car. That means that at the end of the lease, the dealer could value the car much lower and you are responsible for paying the difference in cash immediately. Avoid this type of lease. Don't just walk away from this type of lease, run.

The alternative is a closed-end lease, which is now the most common. Except for excessive mileage and excessive wear and tear, you are not responsible for additional charges at the end of the lease term. If the car is in acceptable condition, you can simply turn it in, having fulfilled your legal commitment. Of the two, this is the only type of lease to consider.

Is Leasing a Good Alternative?

Many people are attracted to leasing for several reasons. Leasing offers a variety of benefits, including lower monthly payments and the potential to avoid a down payment. However, leasing is *not* for everyone. It is important for you to be aware that leasing may have serious financial disadvantages. Leasing may be right for you only if your answers to these questions are all yes.

1. Is your annual income at least twice the list price of the car you intend to lease?
2. Do you have an excellent credit history?
3. Will you drive this car an average of 15,000 miles per year or less?
4. Do you keep your car in pristine condition?
5. Can you realistically and confidently commit to keeping this car for the *entire* term of the lease?

DOES LEASING REQUIRE ANY MONEY UP FRONT?

Although a down payment is usually not required, you will pay the first month's rent and a security deposit in advance. Security deposits are typically as high as the equivalent of one month's rent plus $200. This is the dealer's protection against excessive wear and tear. The security deposit is refundable only if you deliver the car to the dealer in satisfactory condition at the end of the lease term. The determination of satisfactory condition is up to the dealer and is often a point of very heated dispute.

IS A LEASED CAR COVERED UNDER WARRANTY?

Yes. You are covered under the manufacturer's warranty and any extended warranty you purchase. Nonwarranty repairs are solely your responsibility.

WHO PAYS FOR INSURANCE?

You are contractually responsible for insuring the vehicle. In fact, most leases require certain coverages such as:

$50,000 property damage minimum

$100,000–$300,000 bodily injury liability minimum

$500 maximum deductible on comprehensive and collision

HOW DOES HIGH MILEAGE AFFECT THE LEASE?

You may either negotiate a high mileage rate into the lease, or pay penalties when you turn it in. Both options are quite expensive. If you anticipate driving in excess of 15,000 miles annually, you should seriously reconsider if leasing is a good financial decision. Excessive mileage penalties at the end of the lease may be as high as 15 cents per mile. For example, if you put 58,000 miles on your car and your three-year lease allows for 45,000 total miles, you would have to pay a whopping $1,950 for excessive mileage. Alternatively, buying excess miles when you negotiate the lease is preferable and typically costs about eight cents a mile. In the previous example, your 13,000 excess miles would add $1,040 to the total cost of the lease, if negotiated up front.

WHAT IF I WANT TO TERMINATE THE LEASE EARLY?

You run the risk of owing more on the car than it's worth. Simply put, you must come up with the difference in cash to buy yourself out of the contract. Read the contract carefully before you sign it. Don't sign a lease with costly early termination penalties. You could end up paying many thousands of dollars more than you anticipated.

WHAT IF THE LEASED CAR IS STOLEN OR DESTROYED?

Your insurance coverage may or may not be adequate to cover the financial obligations of your lease. Insurance companies generally protect the value of the asset, not the total of the payments of your lease. Unless you have additional insurance to cover the difference, you would have to pay the difference out of your pocket.

WHAT IS CONSIDERED ACCEPTABLE WEAR AND TEAR AT THE END OF THE LEASE?

Read the lease contract very thoroughly. You are responsible for the specific terms related to the car's condition at the end of the lease. Be sure that you have a complete understanding of how the dealer defines acceptable condition, and that it is clearly stated in the contract. Any ambiguities are almost certain to result in a potentially costly conflict for you. Generally, dealers require the following:

- All parts and accessories should be in good working order, including the radio equipment, dashboard gauges and controls, seat belts, electronic accessories, and even the spare tire and tire jack. Anything that came with the car should be returned in good working order. The windows should be functioning properly, without chips or cracks.
- The systems of the car should be in sound running order, including the fuel system, the electrical system, the cooling system, the lubrication system, the exhaust system, the transmission, the brake system, the steering and suspension, the differential and drive shaft, and the engine. For more detail, Chapter 4 outlines the basic components of the car's systems.
- Tires must pass inspection, having at least one-eighth-inch-deep tread and 25 percent of their life remaining.
- Minor paint nicks and door dings may or may not be accept-

able. Any body damage such as dents, holes, and missing or damaged parts will be charged against you. There shouldn't be any body rust visible on the car.

WHAT PROTECTIONS DO CONSUMERS HAVE?

When you lease, you are considered a renter in the eyes of the law. The Consumer Credit Act requires the lessor (dealer) to state:

- that the contract is a lease
- the amount of cash required up front
- the total of all payments and the number of payments required
- your liability for the difference between the estimated and actual market values of the car at the end of the lease
- how the actual market value will be determined at the end of the lease
- if you have an option to purchase the car, and if so, when and at what terms

Be careful. The Consumer Credit Act does not require the lessor to state:

- the actual interest rate being charged
- the lessor's true estimate of the value of the car at the end of the lease
- the actual balance you may owe at the end of the lease

IS LEASING RIGHT FOR YOU?

Many people lease cars and are satisfied customers. These people generally know what they are doing and take the necessary time to do it right. But it's not right for everyone. Only you can decide if it's right for you.

If this section *raised* more questions than it answered, you may want to talk with friends, relatives, and co-workers about their experiences. But be wary of biased sources such as leasing agents or car salesmen. In the end, *you* have to pay for the car and live with it. Do what *you* feel best about.

How Dealers Secretly Scam You

Every year, more than 14 million people in America buy a car or truck from a dealer. It is estimated by car dealers themselves that less than 10 percent of them know what they're doing. The rest lose approximately $4 billion in negotiating the purchase price and another $600 million for add-ons they don't receive or need. You can arm yourself against such losses. New and used car dealers operate similarly in the way they sell cars, but differently in their inventory purchasing methods and costs. New car dealers buy their new car inventory from the car manufacturer at fairly standard predetermined prices. Manufacturers often run promotions for both their dealers and the consumer if sales are lagging or they have excessive inventory. These campaigns are usually widely advertised to the general public and typically involve rebates, incentives, and discounts. To motivate the dealer to sell more cars, manufacturers offer increased profits to the dealer and very attractive financial incentives to the salesmen. That's why we feel so pressured by salespeople. They are highly motivated to earn more money and are under intense pressure from the dealer to close a large number of lucrative sales each month.

Independent used car dealers are generally not so sophisticated in their sales campaigns and techniques. But beware of any dealer who uses the techniques described in this section. In my car dealership, our philosophy is, "We make our profit when we *buy* the car, *not* when we sell it." Meaning that if we buy our inventory *selectively* at the *right* price, we can offer dependable quality at a fair price to our customers.

Independent used car dealers have no manufacturer behind them offering attractive financial incentives for performance. So the sales pressure may be lower or less polished. The down side of that, though, means that no national conglomerate is looking over their shoulder with controls on integrity, quality, and customer service. That's why many independent used car dealers have a poor image and reputation in their community. At my dealership, we are appealing to the consumer who is interested in knowing that the car is a good value, and the purchase price is fair. We openly discuss the pros and cons of the condition and market value of each car. This is the type of consumer who understands that the company must make some reasonable profit on each car sale in order to stay in business, and is looking for a win-win relationship.

Here are dealers' favorite secrets. Each is followed by a suggestion for neutralizing it, allowing you to optimize your negotiating position:

SECRET: On the average, consumers have about three and one-half hours per week of free time. Car salesmen like to use up your time so you'll do less comparative shopping.

SOLUTION: Don't be rushed, pushed, or persuaded. Take your time. Do your homework. If you're not ready, walk away.

SECRET: Car salesmen play off the emotional appeal of owning a new car.

SOLUTION: Don't get sucked in. If you are feeling great emotional desire, don't let the salesman know it. Then, leave and think about it for 48 hours before you sign anything.

SECRET: Some car salesmen are very likable. You feel comfortable and think you can trust them.

SOLUTION: Never forget that the salesman is there for only one purpose, to make money (off you). If a salesman is "nice," don't be fooled. Only *you* will watch out for you.

SECRET: It is the salesman's job to sell you a car *today*, at the highest price, with the most add-ons, at the highest interest rate. This increases the dealer's profit and his commission. Most car salesmen work on straight commission.

SOLUTION: Do your homework. Know the value of the car and decide on specific options *before* you shop. Take your time. Don't buy before comparison shopping. Shop for the best financing.

SECRET: An option or add-on sold for $300 will cost $328 if it's financed at 10 percent for 60 months. Salesmen get you to buy it by pointing out that, "It's only about twenty cents a day. You can afford *that*, can't you?"

SOLUTION: Don't buy options you don't want or need. *Just say no*.

SECRET: New cars may lose 30 percent of their value the moment you drive them off the lot.

SOLUTION: Buy a three- to five-year-old car. Depreciation is minimal and so is your interest expense.

SECRET: Used car lots make money by buying cars at a price that is much lower than wholesale and selling them at retail or greater. You will pay for their profit first.

SOLUTION: Buy a car *only* if the price is at wholesale or below (see page 157 for determining its market value). Only by doing this will you retain equity. Otherwise, the dealer gets your equity in the form of excessive profit.

SECRET: Car dealers also make a good profit on your trade-in. You can be grossly underpaid for your old car. For the dealer this can make up for the "fair" deal you've worked so hard to negotiate on your new car. Overall you may still lose.

SOLUTION: Know the book value of your trade-in. Insist that all components of the negotiation be fair for you. Or, better yet, sell your car yourself. You'll probably get more for it.

SECRET: Salesmen may claim never to discount off sticker price.

SOLUTION: Go somewhere else. Laugh. Walk away.

SECRET: Salesmen claim that a small discount is their rock-bottom price.

SOLUTION: Common pricing methods by new car dealers will generally allow you to use a formula to determine a fair dealer profit. Subtract 15 percent from the sticker price, then add $600. This should come pretty close to the dealer's actual minimum profit of $200. If you can't buy the car for that, walk away.

SECRET: The salesman claims that his offer is a special deal today only.

SOLUTION: If you run into this claim, don't believe it. Consider your salesman a liar and leave.

SECRET: Salesmen will *always* claim that the book value is meaningless, distorted, et cetera.

SOLUTION: Don't believe them. Stick to your guns.

SECRET: The salesman will try to set the price (high), negotiate add-ons and options (many), and give you a package offer on your trade-in (low). He'll concentrate on the monthly payment amount instead of the valuations.

SOLUTION: Determine your offer for a car by finding the value and paying wholesale or less. Don't trade in your car unless you get wholesale or greater. Arrange financing elsewhere.

SECRET: High-volume dealers negotiate car deals 5,000 times each year or more. They're pros.

SOLUTION: Go through the dealer's fleet department. They will play fewer games in negotiating. Or you can seek out a young salesman. They are less experienced and may be more eager to make deals. But beware—they have just spent weeks in training.

SECRET: Shopping at night or on the weekends is the best time for the *dealer*.

SOLUTION: Shop during a weekday at the end of the month, when dealers are more willing to negotiate in order to boost their volume for the month.

SECRET: A salesman's greatest fear is that you will walk away. They may even allow you to drive the vehicle home for the evening to avoid losing you. Beware.

SOLUTION: You *will* gain control when you start to walk away (and mean it). The price will suddenly be more negotiable than the salesman first admitted. *Do this*. It's your *most* powerful tool. If you don't get your price, then *walk away*. And don't settle for less.

SECRET: Consumers have been known to sign contracts that are legally binding, but reflect terms that are different from their understanding.

SOLUTION: Before you sign anything, check all terms and figures. Check that the payment schedule reflects the interest rate you agreed to.

Negotiating Dos and Don'ts

Effective negotiation is an acquired skill. Even if you've never had an opportunity to learn, you can start with these pointers and be well on your way to savvy negotiating, saving lots of time and money. Once you try it, you'll find that it's much easier than you think. These tips emphasize preparation before you begin. Knowledge is power. Savvy negotiating can only begin when you arm yourself with pertinent information. The following list is ordered in a way that follows the buying/negotiation process:

DO: Find out exactly how much your trade-in car is worth before you talk to salespeople.

DO: Look through the classified ads to find prices on comparable cars.

DO: Decide your maximum offer *before* you begin negotiating.

DON'T: Tell them what your motivations are for buying the car. (Don't divulge your decision criteria.)

DO: Make your first offer 20 percent below your maximum offer.

DO: Stay calm and unemotional.

DON'T: Exhibit a strong desire for the car.

DO: Be prepared to walk out *and mean it* anytime you are uncomfortable. As mentioned in the previous section, this is the most important thing you can do to protect yourself.

DON'T: Let the salesman intimidate or pressure you.

DO: Answer a question with a question if the salesman is getting too personal.

DO: Complete the inspection checklists on pages 179–188 before you begin negotiation.

DO: Point out defects, damage, or potential problems to the salesperson.

DO: Make your third offer final.

DON'T: Let the salesman counteroffer more than twice.

DO: Get everything you want included in the deal before you sign it. No one will throw in anything after it is final.

DO: Lead the salesman to believe he will finance the deal. Only after you have agreed on price, tell him you are financing it elsewhere or paying cash. (See pages 171–175.)

DO: Bring a friend or relative on your first outing who is more experienced in car buying and negotiating.

If You Refuse to Negotiate

If you wish to avoid a lengthy negotiating session, many dealers will accept one firm offer rather than lose the deal. After you choose and test drive the car, handle it this way:

> I'm satisfied that this car meets my needs. I'm ready to take delivery *today*, on one condition: I will make *one* firm offer and I will not negotiate. I appreciate your need to make a fair profit, and I am prepared to offer you a profit of $200 over your invoice.

Of course, I will need to see the invoice. If this is not attractive to you, let's not waste any more time. I will go down the street to close the deal with your competitor.

In this scenario, you may get a positive response with a counteroffer of a slightly higher profit. Cut short their attempts to lure you into their negotiating methods. Pick up your belongings and head for the door. If they let you walk, then another dealer will accept your deal. If you agree to a compromise, you *must* be sure to match the vehicle identification number (VIN) on the invoice to the car you are purchasing. Doing this will ensure that the dealer is not showing you another car's invoice to trick you into paying a bigger profit.

Dealership Financing: Is It Right for You?

Eight out of ten people who buy a new car finance it through a dealer.

Dealership financing is not right for everyone. However, if you are a new college graduate with a job, a first-time car buyer, a person with poor credit, minimal credit history, or marginal credit quality; or someone who needs a longer term, or needs lower monthly payments, a dealership may be your best source. You would be wise to compare financing before you negotiate with a dealer. Apply for a loan at a bank or credit union first. Try other financing sources and negotiate their best terms first. Don't sign anything yet. Compare terms, then choose the best for you.

Dealership sources such as GMAC, FMCC, and Chrysler Credit are reputable, though credit unions or banks are generally less expensive. The most threatening aspect, however, is the enormous pressure dealers apply to sell you on their financing package. Remember this: The finance office is the most lucrative department of most dealerships. Their motivation is profit, so they use high-pressure sales tactics. Be careful.

Other Financing Options

Before you negotiate terms with a dealer, compare rates with these sources:

Credit unions:

- Generally charge less for loans than banks
- Are unbiased lenders as to make and model
- Are not motivated by the need to sell cars

Banks:

- Generally charge less for loans than dealer-financed sources
- Generally offer lower car-loan rates to their banking customers
- Are low-pressure salespeople

Home equity line of credit:

- Is available at current mortgage interest rates from banks and mortgage lenders
- Is generally limited to 85 percent of the current appraised value of your home, minus the existing mortgage principal balance
- Should be kept as short term as possible
- May provide tax savings for you
- Remember: Your house is now attached to this debt as a tertiary source of repayment

Cash value in your whole life insurance policy:

- If you have such a policy with cash value
- Ask your agent for the current cash value
- Rates are generally half of rates from other sources
- Set up a monthly repayment plan

This is just a start. Ask your family, friends, and co-workers for their experience and advice. Then consider your options and decide what's right for you.

Save Thousands by Understanding Debt

If you don't have ready cash to buy your new car outright, knowing the basics of financing will save you thousands of dollars.

How much can you afford to finance? As a general rule, you'll pay roughly $25 per month for every $1,000 you finance. Using this guide, financing $17,000 would mean paying $425 per month.

But beware! If you don't know how to protect yourself, you could pay hundreds of dollars a month more than you have to. That means thousands more over the life of the loan.

The keys to saving are: finance at the *lowest* rate possible and finance for the *shortest* term possible.

For example, you buy a new car for $17,000. Your payments and total interest expense could vary widely:

8 percent loans at 24 and 60 months:

Interest rate (APR)	8%	8%
Term—months	24	60
Monthly payment	$ 768.86	$ 344.70
Total of payments	$18,452.64	$20,682.00
Total interest paid	$ 1,452.64	$ 3,682.00

Contrast these with 14 percent loans at 24 and 60 months:

Interest rate (APR)	14%	14%
Term—months	24	60
Monthly payment	$ 816.17	$ 395.42
Total of payments	$19,588.08	$23,725.20
Total interest paid	$ 2,588.08	$ 6,725.20

In this example, you save $5,271.36 by financing the same car at a *lower* rate over a *shorter* term.

Appendix A will help you find your monthly payment, or

your loan officer should be happy to help you calculate variations on your loan. If they pressure you, they don't have *your* best interest in mind. Walk away.

How to Stay Out of the Debt Cycle

Never run into debt;
not if you can find anything else to run into.
                    —JOSH BILLINGS, 1919

Do you owe more on your car than it's worth? Or, if you sold it today at its book value, could you pay off the loan and have money left over? Here's how to find out:

Call your bank or finance company for the
   principal balance on your loan: $ _____

Ask them to look up the current NADA
   Official Used Car Guide value. You must
   give them:

   • Make/model
   • Year
   • Body type
   • Options/mileage $ _____

Subtract the NADA value from the loan
   balance. The result is your positive or
   negative equity: $ _____

Most cars are financed by the "Rule of 78." This means that much more interest is paid at the beginning of the loan. In fact, in the first 12 months of a 60-month loan, 35 percent of the entire interest will be paid. If your payment is fixed, then you will be paying much more interest initially.

This is how dealers make a lot of money.

This is how you are trapped in a cycle of debt.

Many people make payments for their entire lives and never have any equity in their automobiles.

Your objectives should be:

- to pay down your principal balance to achieve positive equity. Make additional principal payments whenever possible. Be sure to state "Additional principal payment" on the check. Follow up to ensure that it was applied to reduce your *principal* balance.
- ultimately, to pay *off* your loan to achieve *no* debt and 100 percent equity.
- to continue to "pay" your savings account the amount you have previously paid your car loan. If you continue to drive your car to 150,000 miles, you will probably save enough to pay for your next car in *cash*.

This will keep you out of the debt cycle that traps millions of Americans.

Make Sure Your Warranty Covers Your Needs

A service contract is different from a warranty. It pays for repairs or maintenance not covered by the warranty. It costs a lot more and is considered an add-on with high profit for the dealer.

NEW CAR WARRANTIES:

Full warranties must comply with federal law, under the Magnuson-Moss Warranty Act:

- Anyone who owns the vehicle in the warranty period is covered.
- Warranty service is free of charge. This includes costs of returning the vehicle and the repairs.

- If the repairs aren't satisfactory after a reasonable number of attempts, the consumer may get a replacement or full refund.
- A warranty registration card is not required.

Be sure to read and understand the warranty. Extended warranties are usually offered in three levels: minimum, average, and maximum. The average package is usually a cost-efficient choice, unless you have special circumstances or needs. Warranties are negotiable as part of the purchase price, and may be discounted by $100 or more. Make a list of your needs. If the warranty doesn't cover them, insist that it be changed or walk away from the deal.

USED CAR WARRANTIES:

Most used cars are sold with extremely limited warranties or "as is." When you buy a car as is, the seller guarantees nothing and you must bear the cost of any problems it has.

Dealers are obligated by law to disclose known defects. Dealers must post a buyers' guide on used cars. These must indicate the type of warranty on the car, and problems that could be present. No two car warranties are the same. Read your warranty thoroughly. Claims made by the salesperson are called "expressed warranties." If you feel they are important, put them in *writing* prior to signing a contract.

10

How to Buy a
Used Car

Why Buy a Used Car?

You can save 50 percent of your automobile costs by driving a
good used car. I've learned that if you do your homework, take
time to find a good car, and fill out the following checklists, the
car you dream about just may be affordable. Buying my Jaguar,
which I mentioned in the introduction, is the perfect example of
how to cut your car costs in half. I had wanted a Jaguar for
years. Of course buying a Jaguar seemed way out of my reach.
Not only are they costly luxury cars, but repairs and maintenance are reputedly very expensive for them, as well.

First, the homework is essential. As I said, new Jaguars really
were out of my financial ballpark. No question about it. So I
began to price used Jags. The used car guides gave me a range
of market values, depending on year, model, condition, mileage, and other options. I found out that I could probably afford
a four- or five-year-old Jag. This was quite exciting, and I began
to watch the classified ads. Any Jag in my price range caught
my attention, and I compared the asking price to my price

guidebooks. If it was reasonable, I called the seller for more information. Sometimes I went to look at it, and sometimes I didn't depending on the description. Even relatively high mileage didn't scare me away, as long as it was meticulously maintained.

I looked for many months. Finding a great car at a great price takes consistent and patient effort. But it is *well* worth it. Sometimes it's tempting to give up and buy something that's not just what you want. You may be frustrated or begin to believe that you'll never find it. Don't give up hope. The car you want is out there, and if you've defined what you want, set your priorities, and done your research, you *will* find it.

I found my Jag eventually through a friend. Getting the word out is an excellent way to multiply your search efforts. Some very good car deals don't ever get into the newspaper. For instance, my friend was going to trade his Jaguar in for a new car. He had bought the Jag new from a local dealer five years ago. It had been a wonderful car for him, but it had over 100,000 miles on it and he wanted a sportier car. He intended to trade it in when he bought a new one.

Even then I thought that his Jag would be out of my reach. The car had been impeccably cared for. All maintenance was performed on schedule and the oil was changed every 3,000 miles. He kept a complete set of the service records. The car was even kept in a garage, both at home and at work. It was beautiful. When he told me what the dealer offered him, I was astounded. It was in my range! And one of the best things about it was that the price was a little under wholesale. So that if I sold it, I could actually make a profit. There are no tricks involved with finding a great used car. You just have to know how to go about it and have patience.

If you're shopping the classified ads or used car dealers, careful inspection and price research are the keys to finding a good car for a good price. You may have to shop dozens of cars before you find a good one. Use the same strategies for decision making, shopping, and negotiating that are outlined in this chapter. Begin negotiation only *after* you have thoroughly completed the following checklists to ensure you are informed and organized when it comes to making a decision.

Used Car Questions to Ask the Seller

The principle of caveat emptor is as American as apple pie. And that means that it's up to *you* to determine the car's history and condition *before* you buy. These questions will help:

- Why is the car being sold?
- Who owned it previously? (Get names and phone numbers. Call them to discuss its pros and cons, if possible.)
- Where was the car serviced?
- Do they have service records you can inspect and take?
- Has it had major repairs?
- Does it *need* any repairs?
- Has it had all scheduled maintenance?
- Was the oil changed every 3,000 miles?
- How many miles does it run before oil must be added?
- Is the odometer correct?
- Has it been driven primarily in the city?
- Has it ever been in an accident?
- Has it been repainted?

Answers to these questions, along with the following inspection checklists, will give you a good idea of the vehicle's condition.

Interior Inspection Checklist

The interior gives you clues to the car's value and condition.

1. If it's been neglected on the inside, it's probably been neglected mechanically, too.

2. Excessive wear may give you a clue that the odometer's been tampered with. Does the wear look consistent with the mileage on the odometer?
3. An attractive car will be more enjoyable for you and easier to resell.

No Problem	Possible Problem	
_____	_____	Seat upholstery clean and in good shape
_____	_____	Carpet not excessively worn
_____	_____	Gas, brake, and clutch pedals operate well
_____	_____	Doors/handles in good working order
_____	_____	No foreign/musty smells
_____	_____	No rust inside/under seats
_____	_____	Glove compartment works
_____	_____	Owner's manual/original warranty inside
_____	_____	Front seats slide smoothly
_____	_____	All windows work well
		Dashboard: Turn ignition to "alt": Dash lights:
_____	_____	Alternator light should go on
_____	_____	Oil pressure light should go on
_____	_____	Emergency blinkers work
_____	_____	Both turn signals work

No Problem	Possible Problem	
————	————	Windshield wipers and washers work
————	————	Heater works
————	————	Air conditioner works
————	————	Fan works
————	————	Horn works
————	————	Clock works
————	————	Parking brake works
————	————	Rear window defogger works
————	————	Sunroof works
————	————	Radio works
		Turn the ignition on:
————	————	Alternator light should go off
————	————	Oil pressure light should go off

Possible problem notes: _____

_____

_____

Exterior Inspection Checklist

Inspect the exterior of the car very carefully. By utilizing this
checklist you can tell if it's been in an accident. If you suspect it
has, ask. *Never* buy a previously wrecked car. If it looks neglected, it probably was. A good daylight inspection can give
you clues.

No Problem	Possible Problem	
_____	_____	All window glass in good shape
		Lights work:
_____	_____	Headlights
_____	_____	Tail lights
_____	_____	Flashers
_____	_____	Backup lights
_____	_____	Brake lights
_____	_____	Turn signals (front and back)
_____	_____	Parking lights
_____	_____	No rust present on outside or in:
_____	_____	Wheel wells
_____	_____	Rain gutters
_____	_____	Window moldings
_____	_____	Door frames
_____	_____	Trim
_____	_____	Undercarriage
_____	_____	Original paint is preferable
_____	_____	All panels same paint shade
_____	_____	All doors work
_____	_____	Driver's door not loose
_____	_____	Gap between door and body not uneven
_____	_____	Hood works
_____	_____	Bumper evenly spaced from body

No Problem	Possible Problem	
_____	_____	Trunk works and:
_____	_____	No musty smells inside
_____	_____	No rust under carpet
_____	_____	Spare is good
_____	_____	Jack works
_____	_____	No leaks under the car
_____	_____	No black/gummy substance inside tailpipe
_____	_____	Tire wear is even
_____	_____	Shocks bounce only once
_____	_____	Car sits level with the ground
_____	_____	Front and rear wheels align

Possible problem notes: _____

_____

_____

Under-the-Hood Inspection Checklist

Checking these simple things will help you avoid lemons or costly problems:

No Problem	Possible Problem	
		Before starting the car, check for:
_____	_____	No oily film in radiator water

No Problem	Possible Problem	
_____	_____	No rust in radiator water
_____	_____	No sludge inside radiator filler neck
_____	_____	No leaks in engine compartment
		Maintenance stickers in or on:
_____	_____	Door frame
_____	_____	Underside of hood
_____	_____	Air filter
_____	_____	Engine compartment
_____	_____	No cracked or loose belts
_____	_____	No frayed or worn tires
		Fluid levels:
_____	_____	Brake fluid
_____	_____	Power steering fluid
_____	_____	Windshield washer fluid
_____	_____	Battery
_____	_____	Air filter clean
		Start the car. After it runs, check for:
		Oil:
_____	_____	Proper level
_____	_____	Clear, amber color
_____	_____	Not gritty or gummy
_____	_____	No bubbles or milky color
_____	_____	No gas smell

No Problem	Possible Problem	
		Automatic transmission fluid:
_____	_____	Proper level
_____	_____	Reddish in color
_____	_____	Not dark brown and sludgy
_____	_____	No burned smell
_____	_____	No metal flecks

Possible problem notes: _____

_____

_____

Test Drive Checklist

You'll want to drive it on:

Bumpy roads
Highways
Town roads

Leave the radio off and check for problems:

No Problem	Possible Problem	
		Front wheels should respond before turning the steering wheel two inches
_____	_____	
		No blue or white exhaust from tailpipe
_____	_____	
_____	_____	Brakes respond well

No Problem	Possible Problem	
_____	_____	Brakes don't pull to one side
_____	_____	Steering doesn't pull to one side
		No unusual engine noises, including:
_____	_____	No pinging
_____	_____	No tapping
_____	_____	No hissing
_____	_____	No groaning
_____	_____	Smooth transmission shifting
_____	_____	No excessively bumpy ride
_____	_____	Heater works
_____	_____	Air conditioner works
		Pull over and let the engine idle:
_____	_____	Consistent engine sound
_____	_____	No tapping noises
_____	_____	Turn off the engine—it should stop immediately

Possible problem notes: _____

_____

_____

Mechanic's Inspection Checklist

Spending $25 to $50 now on a mechanic's inspection before you buy the car could save you hundreds or even thousands of dollars and lots of time and frustration.

1. The AAA Inspection Center is independent, and is available to *nonmembers* as well as members.
2. Most dealers and service shops offer a thorough inspection and diagnosis.
3. Independent mobile units are popping up around the country. One such business in the northeast is called the Auto Critic.

Make sure that you take the car to a mechanic who is *not* associated with the seller. If the seller won't allow it, then *don't buy it*, no matter how "good" the deal is. Use this checklist:

No Problem	*Possible Problem*	
_____	_____	Engine-compression test, including valves and piston rings
_____	_____	Brakes, pads, and brake lines
_____	_____	Front wheel bearings
_____	_____	Shock absorbers
_____	_____	Frame integrity
_____	_____	Exhaust system
_____	_____	Cooling system
_____	_____	Electrical system
_____	_____	Transmission and drive train
_____	_____	Have the mechanic test drive it
_____	_____	Get a written repair estimate (use this in your decision and/or negotiation)

You will also want to find out:
• How does it compare in crash test ratings?

• Has it been recalled for any reason? If so, has the work been done?

Possible problem notes: _____

_____

_____

Be Wise to Odometer Fraud

• Every year, three million used cars have their odometers rolled back an average of 32,000 miles.
• Fifty percent of all leased cars on the market for sale have had their odometers rolled back.
• You could pay $1,000 more than the value of the car due to odometer fraud.
• According to the FBI, odometer fraud costs consumers $4 billion annually.
• Changing a car's odometer is a violation of federal law.
• You can avoid this fraud by carefully checking for signs of tampering and inconsistencies with the mileage:

1. The numbers on the odometer should line up. If not, it may have been rolled back.
2. Look for maintenance records that indicate service dates and mileage. They're often found in the glove compartment, driver's door, or air filter.
3. Check for wear that belies low mileage on the odometer:

   • Foot pedals
   • Carpeting
   • Seats
   • Door handles
   • Ignition switch
   • Steering column paint

4. Check the dashboard for signs of tampering:

   - Scratches
   - Missing screws

5. Check the title and odometer disclosure statement. They should all be clear and legible.
6. Have your mechanic check for signs of high mileage use:

   - Engine compression
   - Worn struts
   - Worn ball joints
   - Transmission problems
   - Engine/transmission leaks
   - Hose leaks

If you believe the car has had its odometer rolled back, by law you have the right to recover the greater of $1,500 or triple the difference between what the car was worth and what you paid for it.

Contact your state attorney general's office in your state capital and ask for the odometer enforcement unit. They may bring suit against the seller on your behalf. If not, you will need to file suit through a private attorney, and bring evidence, which may include the previous owner's statement of mileage or repair records that contradict the odometer reading.

For more information contact:

National Highway Traffic Safety Administration
Odometer Fraud Staff
400 Seventh Street SW
Washington, D.C. 20590

Or call:

Auto Safety Hotline
(800) 424-9393
(or in Washington, D.C., call 366-0123)

▮▮

Sell Your Car the Smart and Savvy Way

Before I became savvy about selling my car, I joined the legions of folks (female *and* male) who lost thousands in the sale. It's common, and it happens more often than not. My mistake was selling my car to a dealer instead of selling it to an individual. Dealers will not pay as much as an individual will, simply because they must sell it to another individual and make a profit. You can sell your car yourself and keep the profit that would otherwise have gone to the dealer. Cutting out the middleman will put more money in your pocket. I only had to learn that lesson the hard way once. By following the guidelines in this chapter, you won't ever have to learn it the hard way.

Make at Least 25 Percent More Selling Your Car

If your car has a book value of $5,000, chances are that a dealer will give you only $3,000 in a trade-in. With a little time and effort, your car could command the full $5,000 from a private buyer. Sell the car *yourself*. Here's how to start:

- Determine your car's average retail value. Call a bank for the NADA book values. This is the most reliable source.
- Don't accept less than "average loan value" if your car is in relatively good condition with reasonable mileage for that year.
- Call your lender for the payoff amount. Ask them for their procedure to pay off the loan and obtain the title. Your buyer will want this immediately.
- Call your state's vehicle licensing department. Ask what their procedure is for transfer of title and tags (license plates).

Get It Ready First

First impressions count! Before you advertise, put your car in top condition. Clean it thoroughly and make it shine. Fix any missing, loose, or broken parts. Your objective is to show your car at its best. If you don't know how to fix it, ask a knowledge-able clerk at a reputable auto parts store. They can often explain how to repair or replace something very simply and inexpensively. If it's not a simple fix, get an idea of what your mechanic should reasonably charge. Then have the work done before you advertise. Also be sure to:

STEAM CLEAN THE ENGINE COMPARTMENT:

- Fix the source of any oil leaks you find
- Use engine degreaser and go to a self-service car wash

WASH THE EXTERIOR:

- Pay attention to cracks and crevices
- Do wheels and wheel wells thoroughly
- Clean inside the doorjamb
- Get the undercarriage, too
- Use chrome cleaner

- Tire dressing makes a big difference
- This may take two to three hours to do a good job

TOUCH UP DINGS AND SCRATCHES:

- Do this before you wax
- Auto parts stores and dealerships carry small tubes or bottles of your paint color
- Use touch-up paint sparingly
- Search for missing trim, dents, or dings and fix them

WAX THE EXTERIOR:

- Apply the best wax you can afford
- Make it shine

CLEAN THE INTERIOR:

- Vacuum well, even under the seats
- Shampoo the carpet, upholstery, and floor mats
- Use a toothbrush to get dirt out of cracks and crevices in the dash, doors, and console
- Clean the ashtrays and glove compartment
- Use a leather or vinyl polish to make it shine
- Clean windows with newspaper to avoid streaks
- Wipe down the ceiling
- Clean the trunk
- Search for missing or broken items, tears, scratches, or breaks and fix them

FIX WORKING PARTS, INCLUDING:

- Air conditioner
- Antenna
- Brake lights
- Clock

- Dashboard lights/gauges
- Doors/Door handles
- Emergency lights
- Headlights
- Heater
- Horn
- Lights (including dome, glove compartment, and license plate)
- Locks
- Mirrors
- Radio
- Spare tire
- Speakers
- Steering wheel tilt
- Taillights
- Tire jack
- Turn signals
- Windshield wipers/blades
- Windshield washer/fluid

INSPECT THE ENGINE COMPARTMENT:

- Fix loose wires
- Check hoses
- Check belts
- Check battery fluid
- Check battery terminals
- Fill fluid reservoirs
- Replace air filter

CHECK AND CHANGE FLUIDS:

- Change engine oil and filter
- Check automatic transmission fluid
- Change coolant

DON'T FORGET:

- Fix rattles and squeaks
- Oil the door, hood, and trunk hinges

HAVE YOUR DOCUMENTS READY:

- Owner's manual
- Service records
- Warranty or service contracts
- Current title
- Registration papers

REPAIRS:

If you do not want to go to the expense of making major repairs, at least be honest about them. Answer buyers' questions honestly and allow a potential buyer to have their mechanic inspect the car.

Advertise for Results

FIRST, PRICE IT RIGHT:

- It should be advertised at 10–15 percent above your rock-bottom acceptable price
- Your rock-bottom price should be no less than "average loan value" if in good condition with reasonable mileage
- The 10–15 percent will give you room to negotiate
- All used car buyers will expect to negotiate
- Many used car buyers are familiar with the book value

PLACES TO ADVERTISE:

- Metropolitan newspapers
- Community newspapers
- Automobile "traders"
- Employee publications
- Local merchant bulletin boards
- Churches or credit unions
- Sign in your car window

YOUR AD SHOULD INCLUDE:

- Make/model
- Year
- Mileage—if low
- Condition
- Important features—stress strong, appealing, emotional points such as color, comfort, and attractive options or distinctions
- Price (10–15 percent above your rock bottom)
- Your phone number and times to call

TIPS:

- Look in your paper's classified section for examples of good ads
- Make your ad different and more interesting
- Have an answering machine record messages
- Keep a list of *all* your car's features by the phone in order to answer questions
- Let everyone who may answer the phone know about the ad and list of features
- Answer all questions honestly but be positive
- Suggest to buyers that they come to see it and set up an appointment for a specific time at a public place

SHOWING YOUR CAR:

- Don't be surprised if some people don't show up
- Be sure to meet them at a busy public place (not your home)
- Bring along a friend, preferably a man
- Make sure you both go with them on the test drive
- Point out special features
- Sell on emotion and back it up with facts: "It's a really nice, comfortable car that I have loved, and it's very reliable"
- They may want their mechanic to check it out

Easy Negotiating

If they're interested after driving it, they may either make an initial offer, or ask your rock-bottom price.

If they make an offer, you can accept it, reject it, or counter at slightly below your asking price (above your rock-bottom price).

If they ask your rock-bottom price, give them a price that you'd consider a home run. Then stay quiet! If they protest, then ask what they'd be willing to offer. You can either accept it, reject it, or counter and negotiate from there.

Example:

Your five-year-old, two-door, subcompact coupe with front-wheel drive, automatic transmission, power sunroof, power windows and door locks, cruise control, AM/FM stereo with cassette deck, and leather interior has 73,500 miles on it. According to the bank's NADA book, the range of book values for this package is:

Average Loan Value $5,100
   Represents the average amount of credit that may be obtained from financing institutions.

Average Trade-in Value $5,500
  Represents latest average wholesale values based on auction
  reports and dealer wholesale reports throughout the region.

Average Retail Value $6,600
  Represents the latest average retail values based on actual
  sales reports from new and used car dealers throughout the
  region.

You've decided that your rock-bottom acceptable price is
$5,500. You've advertised your car at $6,300, which is almost 15
percent more than your rock-bottom price, but still less than
average retail value.

   After exchanging business cards and going for a test drive,
Sam is interested in buying your car:

SAM: "What's the lowest offer you'd take for it?"

YOU: "Well, Sam, I'm asking sixty-three hundred. That's already a discount off retail. Any lot would charge at least that.
   This car is in such good shape that it'll sell for sixty-three
   hundred." (You know better than to give your rock-bottom
   price right away.)

SAM: "Maybe. But it does have some body dings and the
   brakes sound as though they need work. That'll cost me
   several hundred dollars, at least." (Sam is savvy enough to
   point out defects he noticed in his inspection.)

YOU: "So, perhaps that warrants a bigger discount. But I have
   all the service records and you can see for yourself that it's a
   solid, dependable car; a rarity in the used car market. It'll be
   snapped up in no time. But, if you're prepared to finalize the
   transaction *today*, I'd consider letting it go for sixty-one hundred." (Now you stay quiet.)

SAM: "Sixty-one hundred dollars! That's too much. Why,
   brakes alone will be two hundred bucks, and the new
   model year is only two months away. This car will depreci-
   ate ten percent when that comes." (Sam's strong reaction is

a predictable tactic to get the price down even further. Stay strong yourself.)

You: "You're only the second person to look at it. It's a fine car and it'll serve someone very well for years. I'd love to sell it to you today, but you have to see that it's worth what I'm asking. What offer do you have in mind?" (If it's attractive, take it. If it's not, then reject it or carry on negotiations.)

SAM: "I'd give you a certified check today for five thousand eight hundred dollars." (Now it's Sam's turn to be silent.)

You: "Six thousand and it's yours." (Don't come down as much as he comes up!)

SAM: "Well, I don't know. Maybe I should sleep on it. There was another car for fifty-two hundred that I really liked, too, and it had fewer miles on it. (Now Sam is threatening to walk away. This is when he attempts to take control.)

You: "I think you should certainly be sure that the car you're buying is the right one for you. I don't know what condition the other car is in, but I *do* know what condition this one is in. You'll be happy with it. And you know, with used cars, some surprise repair could cost you a lot more than you saved by buying the cheaper car. I'll tell you what. You've driven a hard bargain. For six thousand, I'll throw in the metric tools if you'd like them." (You've refocused the interaction away from price to satisfaction. By standing firm and throwing in the tools, you've given him a gracious way to accept your price.)

SAM: "What about the bike rack?"

You: "That was a gift to my youngest son. I'm afraid it's not mine to give. But I know where you can get one if you really like it. Do we have a deal?" (You've politely declined and asked for the close—at *your* price.)

SAM: "Yes, I believe we do!"

You: "Congratulations! For six thousand by certified check today, you'll be the proud owner of this great car—and the metric tools. I know you'll be pleased. You just made a fine deal." (You repeated the deal, reinforced his decision, and shook hands.)

More Tips:

• Get their name and phone number for future reference.
• Don't give your rock-bottom price over the phone before they've seen the car.
• Point out that dealers ask more for a comparable vehicle.
• Once you've agreed upon a price, repeat the agreement and the price, then shake hands.
• Read on to find out how to lock in the sale and protect yourself, as a handshake is *not* enough.

Payment and Paperwork

Protect yourself:

• If they do not have full payment on the spot, ask for a 10 percent nonrefundable deposit *now*. You may write out a receipt for this. Specify "nonrefundable," and the specific date, time, and place of the transaction to pay in full.
• Keep the vehicle until you receive full payment.
• *Never* accept anything but cash or a certified check for payment in full.
• Write out a sales receipt. Both parties should sign it (see below).
• Do not give them the receipt until you have payment *in full*.

The sales receipt should include:

• Name and address of buyer and seller
• Vehicle make, model, year, and description
• Vehicle identification number (usually on the driver's side of the dash or under the hood)

- Purchase price
- Date
- Sold in "as is" condition
- Both signatures
- Make a copy for the buyer and keep the original

More paperwork:
Your state Department of Motor Vehicles (DMV) has specific requirements for transferring title. They usually are:

- Sign and date the title on the back exactly as it is printed on the front before giving it to the buyer.
- Notify the DMV. This will protect you from any liability for tickets or accidents after you sell the car.
- Don't let the license plates go with the car unless your state specifically allows it.

A Final Word

Now that I have some experience in the world of cars, run my own car dealership, and consider myself savvy, I don't generally fret when a new car challenge arises. I trust my senses, probe my resource texts, and in cases where something is wrong with the car, discuss the symptoms with friends and family. Asking knowledgeable family, friends, or co-workers is one of the savviest things you can do. You'll learn a lot, and most people love to help with advice if they've had a similar experience. You don't have to be experienced with cars to be savvy. And you don't have to know all about how cars work. Most of the basic information is right here, as a ready reference when you need it.

To this day, my father asks about my car: "How's it running? How many miles do you have on it? Is it using any oil?" Most of the time, it seems fine. But when it acts peculiar and I can't seem to pinpoint it, I like to describe the symptoms and ask his advice. Each time, I find out something I didn't know before. You may have a trusted family member or friend who could be an invaluable resource in the world of cars. All it takes to cultivate that relationship is an expression of interest on your part. Ask a few questions about their experiences with car repairs. Ask for their advice on how to save money or who they trust to work on their car. Some of the best advice comes from people who have been unhappy with car service and can help you avoid unnecessary grief, expense, and wasted time.

Throughout my car research and discussions with all types of people, one reaction prevailed: "That's a book men could use, too!" Many men confided that they would buy it for the woman in their life in order to read it themselves. I've learned that as much as they would like us to believe that the car world is a sacred male domain it's just not so. Anyone with the desire and information can easily become car savvy. In fact, you may wish to deliberately leave a copy of *The Savvy Woman's Guide to Cars* on the coffee table for others to pick up, both female *and* male. You may be surprised by the interest it generates from everyone, including the male car buffs you know!

Happy, savvy motoring!

APPENDIX A

Monthly Payment Tables

MONTHLY PAYMENTS FOR 24-MONTH CONVENTIONAL LOANS

Loan Amt.	8.00%	8.25%	8.50%	8.75%	9.00%	9.25%	9.50%	9.75%
$ 500	22.61	22.67	22.73	22.79	22.84	22.90	22.96	23.01
1,000	45.23	45.34	45.46	45.57	45.68	45.80	45.91	46.03
1,500	67.84	68.01	68.18	68.36	68.53	68.70	68.87	69.04
2,000	90.45	90.68	90.91	91.14	91.37	91.60	91.83	92.06
2,500	113.07	113.35	113.64	113.93	114.21	114.50	114.79	115.07
3,000	135.68	136.02	136.37	136.71	137.05	137.40	137.74	138.09
3,500	158.30	158.69	159.09	159.50	159.90	160.30	160.70	161.10
4,000	180.91	181.37	181.82	182.28	182.74	183.20	183.66	184.12
4,500	203.52	204.04	204.55	205.07	205.58	206.10	206.62	207.13
5,000	226.14	226.71	227.28	227.85	228.42	229.00	229.57	230.15
5,500	248.75	249.38	250.01	250.64	251.27	251.90	252.53	253.16
6,000	271.36	272.05	272.73	273.42	274.11	274.80	275.49	276.18
6,500	293.98	294.72	295.46	296.21	296.95	297.70	298.44	299.19
7,000	316.59	317.39	318.19	318.99	319.79	320.60	321.40	322.21
7,500	339.20	340.06	340.92	341.78	342.64	343.50	344.36	345.22
8,000	361.82	362.73	363.65	364.56	365.48	366.40	367.32	368.24
8,500	384.43	385.40	386.37	387.35	388.32	389.30	390.27	391.25
9,000	407.05	408.07	409.10	410.13	411.16	412.20	413.23	414.27
9,500	429.66	430.74	431.83	432.92	434.01	435.10	436.19	437.28
10,000	452.27	453.41	454.56	455.70	456.85	458.00	459.14	460.30
10,500	474.89	476.08	477.28	478.49	479.69	480.90	482.10	483.31
11,000	497.50	498.76	500.01	501.27	502.53	503.79	505.06	506.33
11,500	520.11	521.43	522.74	524.06	525.37	526.69	528.02	529.34
12,000	542.73	544.10	545.47	546.84	548.22	549.59	550.97	552.36
12,500	565.34	566.77	568.20	569.63	571.06	572.49	573.93	575.37
13,000	587.95	589.44	590.92	592.41	593.90	595.39	596.89	598.39
13,500	610.57	612.11	613.65	615.20	616.74	618.29	619.85	621.40
14,000	633.18	634.78	636.38	637.98	639.59	641.19	642.80	644.41
14,500	655.80	657.45	659.11	660.77	662.43	664.09	665.76	667.43
15,000	678.41	680.12	681.84	683.55	685.27	686.99	688.72	690.44
15,500	701.02	702.79	704.56	706.34	708.11	709.89	711.67	713.46
16,000	723.64	725.46	727.29	729.12	730.96	732.79	734.63	736.47
16,500	746.25	748.13	750.02	751.91	753.80	755.69	757.59	759.49
17,000	768.86	770.80	772.75	774.69	776.64	778.59	780.55	782.50
17,500	791.48	793.47	795.47	797.48	799.48	801.49	803.50	805.52
18,000	814.09	816.15	818.20	820.26	822.33	824.39	826.46	828.53
18,500	836.70	838.82	840.93	843.05	845.17	847.29	849.42	851.55
19,000	859.32	861.49	863.66	865.83	868.01	870.19	872.38	874.56
19,500	881.93	884.16	886.39	888.62	890.85	893.09	895.33	897.58

10.00%	10.25%	10.50%	10.75%	11.00%	11.25%	11.50%	11.75%
23.07	23.13	23.19	23.25	23.30	23.36	23.42	23.48
46.14	46.26	46.38	46.49	46.61	46.72	46.84	46.96
69.22	69.39	69.56	69.74	69.91	70.09	70.26	70.44
92.29	92.52	92.75	92.98	93.22	93.45	93.68	93.91
115.36	115.65	115.94	116.23	116.52	116.81	117.10	117.39
138.43	138.78	139.13	139.48	139.82	140.17	140.52	140.87
161.51	161.91	162.32	162.72	163.13	163.53	163.94	164.35
184.58	185.04	185.50	185.97	186.43	186.90	187.36	187.83
207.65	208.17	208.69	209.21	209.74	210.26	210.78	211.31
230.72	231.30	231.88	232.46	233.04	233.62	234.20	234.78
253.80	254.43	255.07	255.71	256.34	256.98	257.62	258.26
276.87	277.56	278.26	278.95	279.65	280.34	281.04	281.74
299.94	300.69	301.44	302.20	302.95	303.71	304.46	305.22
323.01	323.82	324.63	325.44	326.25	327.07	327.88	328.70
346.09	346.95	347.82	348.69	349.56	350.43	351.30	352.18
369.16	370.08	371.01	371.93	372.86	373.79	374.72	375.65
392.23	393.21	394.20	395.18	396.17	397.15	398.14	399.13
415.30	416.34	417.38	418.43	419.47	420.52	421.56	422.61
438.38	439.47	440.57	441.67	442.77	443.88	444.98	446.09
461.45	462.60	463.76	464.92	466.08	467.24	468.40	469.57
484.52	485.73	486.95	488.16	489.38	490.60	491.82	493.05
507.59	508.86	510.14	511.41	512.69	513.96	515.24	516.52
530.67	531.99	533.32	534.66	535.99	537.33	538.66	540.00
553.74	555.12	556.51	557.90	559.29	560.69	562.08	563.48
576.81	578.25	579.70	581.15	582.60	584.05	585.50	586.96
599.88	601.39	602.89	604.39	605.90	607.41	608.92	610.44
622.96	624.52	626.08	627.64	629.21	630.77	632.34	633.92
646.03	647.65	649.26	650.89	652.51	654.14	655.76	657.40
669.10	670.78	672.45	674.13	675.81	677.50	679.18	680.87
692.17	693.91	695.64	697.38	699.12	700.86	702.60	704.35
715.25	717.04	718.83	720.62	722.42	724.22	726.02	727.83
738.32	740.17	742.02	743.87	745.73	747.58	749.45	751.31
761.39	763.30	765.20	767.12	769.03	770.95	772.87	774.79
784.46	786.43	788.39	790.36	792.33	794.31	796.29	798.27
807.54	809.56	811.58	813.61	815.64	817.67	819.71	821.74
830.61	832.69	834.77	836.85	838.94	841.03	843.13	845.22
853.68	855.82	857.96	860.10	862.25	864.39	866.55	868.70
876.75	878.95	881.14	883.35	885.55	887.76	889.97	892.18
899.83	902.08	904.33	906.59	908.85	911.12	913.39	915.66

MONTHLY PAYMENTS FOR 24-MONTH CONVENTIONAL LOANS (*continued*)

Loan Amt.	8.00%	8.25%	8.50%	8.75%	9.00%	9.25%	9.50%	9.75%
20,000	904.55	906.83	909.11	911.40	913.69	915.99	918.29	920.59
20,500	927.16	929.50	931.84	934.19	936.54	938.89	941.25	943.61
21,000	949.77	952.17	954.57	956.97	959.38	961.79	964.20	966.62
21,500	972.39	974.84	977.30	979.76	982.22	984.69	987.16	989.64
22,000	995.00	997.51	1,000.02	1,002.54	1,005.06	1,007.59	1,010.12	1,012.65
22,500	1,017.61	1,020.18	1,022.75	1,025.33	1,027.91	1,030.49	1,033.08	1,035.67
23,000	1,040.23	1,042.85	1,045.48	1,048.11	1,050.75	1,053.39	1,056.03	1,058.68
23,500	1,062.84	1,065.52	1,068.21	1,070.90	1,073.59	1,076.29	1,078.99	1,081.70
24,000	1,085.45	1,088.19	1,090.94	1,093.68	1,096.43	1,099.19	1,101.95	1,104.71
24,500	1,108.07	1,110.86	1,113.66	1,116.47	1,119.28	1,122.09	1,124.91	1,127.73
25,000	1,130.68	1,133.53	1,136.39	1,139.25	1,142.12	1,144.99	1,147.86	1,150.74
25,500	1,153.30	1,156.21	1,159.12	1,162.04	1,164.96	1,167.89	1,170.82	1,173.76
26,000	1,175.91	1,178.88	1,181.85	1,184.82	1,187.80	1,190.79	1,193.78	1,196.77
26,500	1,198.52	1,201.55	1,204.58	1,207.61	1,210.65	1,213.69	1,216.73	1,219.79
27,000	1,221.14	1,224.22	1,227.30	1,230.39	1,233.49	1,236.59	1,239.69	1,242.80
27,500	1,243.75	1,246.89	1,250.03	1,253.18	1,256.33	1,259.49	1,262.65	1,265.81
28,000	1,266.36	1,269.56	1,272.76	1,275.96	1,279.17	1,282.39	1,285.61	1,288.83
28,500	1,288.98	1,292.23	1,295.49	1,298.75	1,302.02	1,305.29	1,308.56	1,311.84
29,000	1,311.59	1,314.90	1,318.21	1,321.53	1,324.86	1,328.19	1,331.52	1,334.86
29,500	1,334.21	1,337.57	1,340.94	1,344.32	1,347.70	1,351.09	1,354.48	1,357.87
30,000	1,356.82	1,360.24	1,363.67	1,367.10	1,370.54	1,373.99	1,377.43	1,380.89
30,500	1,379.43	1,382.91	1,386.40	1,389.89	1,393.38	1,396.89	1,400.39	1,403.90
31,000	1,402.05	1,405.58	1,409.13	1,412.67	1,416.23	1,419.79	1,423.35	1,426.92
31,500	1,424.66	1,428.25	1,431.85	1,435.46	1,439.07	1,442.69	1,446.31	1,449.93
32,000	1,447.27	1,450.92	1,454.58	1,458.24	1,461.91	1,465.59	1,469.26	1,472.95
32,500	1,469.89	1,473.60	1,477.31	1,481.03	1,484.75	1,488.48	1,492.22	1,495.96
33,000	1,492.50	1,496.27	1,500.04	1,503.81	1,507.60	1,511.39	1,515.18	1,518.98
33,500	1,515.11	1,518.94	1,522.77	1,526.60	1,530.44	1,534.28	1,538.14	1,541.99
34,000	1,537.73	1,541.61	1,545.49	1,549.38	1,553.28	1,557.18	1,561.09	1,565.01
34,500	1,560.34	1,564.28	1,568.22	1,572.17	1,576.12	1,580.08	1,584.05	1,588.02
35,000	1,582.96	1,586.95	1,590.95	1,594.95	1,598.97	1,602.98	1,607.01	1,611.04

10.00%	10.25%	10.50%	10.75%	11.00%	11.25%	11.50%	11.75%
922.90	925.21	927.52	929.84	932.16	934.48	936.81	939.14
945.97	948.34	950.71	953.08	955.46	957.84	960.23	962.61
969.04	971.47	973.90	976.33	978.76	981.20	983.65	986.09
992.12	994.60	997.08	999.57	1,002.07	1,004.57	1,007.07	1,009.57
1,015.19	1,017.73	1,020.27	1,022.82	1,025.37	1,027.93	1,030.49	1,033.05
1,038.26	1,040.86	1,043.46	1,046.07	1,048.68	1,051.29	1,053.91	1,056.53
1,061.33	1,063.99	1,066.65	1,069.31	1,071.98	1,074.65	1,077.33	1,080.01
1,084.41	1,087.12	1,089.84	1,092.56	1,095.28	1,098.01	1,100.75	1,103.49
1,107.48	1,110.25	1,113.02	1,115.80	1,118.59	1,121.38	1,124.17	1,126.96
1,130.55	1,133.38	1,136.21	1,139.05	1,141.89	1,144.74	1,147.59	1,150.44
1,153.62	1,156.51	1,159.40	1,162.30	1,165.20	1,168.10	1,171.01	1,173.92
1,176.70	1,179.64	1,182.59	1,185.54	1,188.50	1,191.46	1,194.43	1,197.40
1,199.77	1,202.77	1,205.78	1,208.79	1,211.80	1,214.82	1,217.85	1,220.88
1,222.84	1,225.90	1,228.97	1,232.03	1,235.11	1,238.19	1,241.27	1,244.36
1,245.91	1,249.03	1,252.15	1,255.28	1,258.41	1,261.55	1,264.69	1,267.83
1,268.99	1,272.16	1,275.34	1,278.53	1,281.72	1,284.91	1,288.11	1,291.31
1,292.06	1,295.29	1,298.53	1,301.77	1,305.02	1,308.27	1,311.53	1,314.79
1,315.13	1,318.42	1,321.72	1,325.02	1,328.32	1,331.63	1,334.95	1,338.27
1,338.20	1,341.55	1,344.91	1,348.26	1,351.63	1,355.00	1,358.37	1,361.75
1,361.28	1,364.68	1,368.09	1,371.51	1,374.93	1,378.36	1,381.79	1,385.23
1,384.35	1,387.81	1,391.28	1,394.76	1,398.24	1,401.72	1,405.21	1,408.70
1,407.42	1,410.94	1,414.47	1,418.00	1,421.54	1,425.08	1,428.63	1,432.18
1,430.49	1,434.07	1,437.66	1,441.25	1,444.84	1,448.44	1,452.05	1,455.66
1,453.57	1,457.20	1,460.85	1,464.49	1,468.15	1,471.81	1,475.47	1,479.14
1,476.64	1,480.33	1,484.03	1,487.74	1,491.45	1,495.17	1,498.89	1,502.62
1,499.71	1,503.46	1,507.22	1,510.99	1,514.75	1,518.53	1,522.31	1,526.10
1,522.78	1,526.59	1,530.41	1,534.23	1,538.06	1,541.89	1,545.73	1,549.57
1,545.86	1,549.72	1,553.60	1,557.48	1,561.36	1,565.25	1,569.15	1,573.05
1,568.93	1,572.85	1,576.79	1,580.72	1,584.67	1,588.62	1,592.57	1,596.53
1,592.00	1,595.98	1,599.97	1,603.97	1,607.97	1,611.98	1,615.99	1,620.01
1,615.07	1,619.11	1,623.16	1,627.21	1,631.27	1,635.34	1,639.41	1,643.49

MONTHLY PAYMENTS FOR 24-MONTH CONVENTIONAL LOANS (*continued*)

Loan Amt.	12.00%	12.25%	12.50%	12.75%	13.00%	13.25%	13.50%	13.75%
$ 500	23.54	23.60	23.65	23.71	23.77	23.83	23.89	23.95
1,000	47.07	47.19	47.31	47.42	47.54	47.66	47.78	47.89
1,500	70.61	70.79	70.96	71.14	71.31	71.49	71.67	71.84
2,000	94.15	94.38	94.61	94.85	95.08	95.32	95.55	95.79
2,500	117.68	117.98	118.27	118.56	118.85	119.15	119.44	119.74
3,000	141.22	141.57	141.92	142.27	142.63	142.98	143.33	143.68
3,500	164.76	165.17	165.58	165.99	166.40	166.81	167.22	167.63
4,000	188.29	188.76	189.23	189.70	190.17	190.64	191.11	191.58
4,500	211.83	212.36	212.88	213.41	213.94	214.47	215.00	215.53
5,000	235.37	235.95	236.54	237.12	237.71	238.30	238.89	239.47
5,500	258.90	259.55	260.19	260.83	261.48	262.13	262.77	263.42
6,000	282.44	283.14	283.84	284.55	285.25	285.96	286.66	287.37
6,500	305.98	306.74	307.50	308.26	309.02	309.79	310.55	311.32
7,000	329.51	330.33	331.15	331.97	332.79	333.62	334.44	335.26
7,500	353.05	353.93	354.80	355.68	356.56	357.45	358.33	359.21
8,000	376.59	377.52	378.46	379.40	380.33	381.27	382.22	383.16
8,500	400.12	401.12	402.11	403.11	404.11	405.10	406.10	407.11
9,000	423.66	424.71	425.77	426.82	427.88	428.93	429.99	431.05
9,500	447.20	448.31	449.42	450.53	451.65	452.76	453.88	455.00
10,000	470.73	471.90	473.07	474.24	475.42	476.59	477.77	478.95
10,500	494.27	495.50	496.73	497.96	499.19	500.42	501.66	502.90
11,000	517.81	519.09	520.38	521.67	522.96	524.25	525.55	526.84
11,500	541.34	542.69	544.03	545.38	546.73	548.08	549.44	550.79
12,000	564.88	566.28	567.69	569.09	570.50	571.91	573.32	574.74
12,500	588.42	589.88	591.34	592.81	594.27	595.74	597.21	598.69
13,000	611.96	613.47	615.00	616.52	618.04	619.57	621.10	622.63
13,500	635.49	637.07	638.65	640.23	641.81	643.40	644.99	646.58
14,000	659.03	660.66	662.30	663.94	665.59	667.23	668.88	670.53
14,500	682.57	684.26	685.96	687.65	689.36	691.06	692.77	694.48
15,000	706.10	707.85	709.61	711.37	713.13	714.89	716.66	718.42
15,500	729.64	731.45	733.26	735.08	736.90	738.72	740.54	742.37
16,000	753.18	755.04	756.92	758.79	760.67	762.55	764.43	766.32
16,500	776.71	778.64	780.57	782.50	784.44	786.38	788.32	790.27
17,000	800.25	802.24	804.22	806.22	808.21	810.21	812.21	814.21
17,500	823.79	825.83	827.88	829.93	831.98	834.04	836.10	838.16
18,000	847.32	849.43	851.53	853.64	855.75	857.87	859.99	862.11
18,500	870.86	873.02	875.19	877.35	879.52	881.70	883.87	886.05
19,000	894.40	896.62	898.84	901.07	903.29	905.53	907.76	910.00
19,500	917.93	920.21	922.49	924.78	927.07	929.36	931.65	933.95

Loan Amt.	12.00%	12.25%	12.50%	12.75%	13.00%	13.25%	13.50%	13.75%
20,000	941.47	943.81	946.15	948.49	950.84	953.19	955.54	957.90
20,500	965.01	967.40	969.80	972.20	974.61	977.02	979.43	981.84
21,000	988.54	991.00	993.45	995.91	998.38	1,000.85	1,003.32	1,005.79
21,500	1,012.08	1,014.59	1,017.11	1,019.63	1,022.15	1,024.68	1,027.21	1,029.74
22,000	1,035.62	1,038.19	1,040.76	1,043.34	1,045.92	1,048.51	1,051.09	1,053.69
22,500	1,059.15	1,061.78	1,064.41	1,067.05	1,069.69	1,072.34	1,074.98	1,077.63
23,000	1,082.69	1,085.38	1,088.07	1,090.76	1,093.46	1,096.16	1,098.87	1,101.58
23,500	1,106.23	1,108.97	1,111.72	1,114.48	1,117.23	1,119.99	1,122.76	1,125.53
24,000	1,129.76	1,132.57	1,135.38	1,138.19	1,141.00	1,143.82	1,146.65	1,149.48
24,500	1,153.30	1,156.16	1,159.03	1,161.90	1,164.77	1,167.65	1,170.54	1,173.42
25,000	1,176.84	1,179.76	1,182.68	1,185.61	1,188.55	1,191.48	1,194.43	1,197.37
25,500	1,200.37	1,203.35	1,206.34	1,209.32	1,212.32	1,215.31	1,218.31	1,221.32
26,000	1,223.91	1,226.95	1,229.99	1,233.04	1,236.09	1,239.14	1,242.20	1,245.27
26,500	1,247.45	1,250.54	1,253.64	1,256.75	1,259.86	1,262.97	1,266.09	1,269.21
27,000	1,270.98	1,274.14	1,277.30	1,280.46	1,283.63	1,286.80	1,289.98	1,293.16
27,500	1,294.52	1,297.73	1,300.95	1,304.17	1,307.40	1,310.63	1,313.87	1,317.11
28,000	1,318.06	1,321.33	1,324.60	1,327.89	1,331.17	1,334.46	1,337.76	1,341.06
28,500	1,341.59	1,344.92	1,348.26	1,351.60	1,354.94	1,358.29	1,361.64	1,365.00
29,000	1,365.13	1,368.52	1,371.91	1,375.31	1,378.71	1,382.12	1,385.53	1,388.95
29,500	1,388.67	1,392.11	1,395.57	1,399.02	1,402.48	1,405.95	1,409.42	1,412.90
30,000	1,412.20	1,415.71	1,419.22	1,422.73	1,426.25	1,429.78	1,433.31	1,436.85
30,500	1,435.74	1,439.30	1,442.87	1,446.45	1,450.03	1,453.61	1,457.20	1,460.79
31,000	1,459.28	1,462.90	1,466.53	1,470.16	1,473.80	1,477.44	1,481.09	1,484.74
31,500	1,482.81	1,486.49	1,490.18	1,493.87	1,497.57	1,501.27	1,504.98	1,508.69
32,000	1,506.35	1,510.09	1,513.83	1,517.58	1,521.34	1,525.10	1,528.86	1,532.64
32,500	1,529.89	1,533.68	1,537.49	1,541.30	1,545.11	1,548.93	1,552.75	1,556.58
33,000	1,553.42	1,557.28	1,561.14	1,565.01	1,568.88	1,572.76	1,576.64	1,580.53
33,500	1,576.96	1,580.88	1,584.79	1,588.72	1,592.65	1,596.59	1,600.53	1,604.48
34,000	1,600.50	1,604.47	1,608.45	1,612.43	1,616.42	1,620.42	1,624.42	1,628.43
34,500	1,624.03	1,628.07	1,632.10	1,636.14	1,640.19	1,644.25	1,648.31	1,652.37
35,000	1,647.57	1,651.66	1,655.76	1,659.86	1,663.96	1,668.08	1,672.20	1,676.32

MONTHLY PAYMENT FOR 36-MONTH CONVENTIONAL LOANS

Loan Amt.	8.00%	8.25%	8.50%	8.75%	9.00%	9.25%	9.50%	9.75%
$ 500	15.67	15.73	15.78	15.84	15.90	15.96	16.02	16.07
1,000	31.34	31.45	31.57	31.68	31.80	31.92	32.03	32.15
1,500	47.00	47.18	47.35	47.53	47.70	47.87	48.05	48.22
2,000	62.67	62.90	63.14	63.37	63.60	63.83	64.07	64.30
2,500	78.34	78.63	78.92	79.21	79.50	79.79	80.08	80.37
3,000	94.01	94.36	94.70	95.05	95.40	95.75	96.10	96.45
3,500	109.68	110.08	110.49	110.89	111.30	111.71	112.12	112.52
4,000	125.35	125.81	126.27	126.73	127.20	127.66	128.13	128.60
4,500	141.01	141.53	142.05	142.58	143.10	143.62	144.15	144.67
5,000	156.68	157.26	157.84	158.42	159.00	159.58	160.16	160.75
5,500	172.35	172.99	173.62	174.26	174.90	175.54	176.18	176.82
6,000	188.02	188.71	189.41	190.10	190.80	191.50	192.20	192.90
6,500	203.69	204.44	205.19	205.94	206.70	207.46	208.21	208.97
7,000	219.35	220.16	220.97	221.78	222.60	223.41	224.23	225.05
7,500	235.02	235.89	236.76	237.63	238.50	239.37	240.25	241.12
8,000	250.69	251.61	252.54	253.47	254.40	255.33	256.26	257.20
8,500	266.36	267.34	268.32	269.31	270.30	271.29	272.28	273.27
9,000	282.03	283.07	284.11	285.15	286.20	287.25	288.30	289.35
9,500	297.70	298.79	299.89	300.99	302.10	303.20	304.31	305.42
10,000	313.36	314.52	315.68	316.84	318.00	319.16	320.33	321.50
10,500	329.03	330.24	331.46	332.68	333.90	335.12	336.35	337.57
11,000	344.70	345.97	347.24	348.52	349.80	351.08	352.36	353.65
11,500	360.37	361.70	363.03	364.36	365.70	367.04	368.38	369.72
12,000	376.04	377.42	378.81	380.20	381.60	382.99	384.40	385.80
12,500	391.70	393.15	394.59	396.04	397.50	398.95	400.41	401.87
13,000	407.37	408.87	410.38	411.89	413.40	414.91	416.43	417.95
13,500	423.04	424.60	426.16	427.73	429.30	430.87	432.44	434.02
14,000	438.71	440.33	441.95	443.57	445.20	446.83	448.46	450.10
14,500	454.38	456.05	457.73	459.41	461.10	462.79	464.48	466.17
15,000	470.05	471.78	473.51	475.25	477.00	478.74	480.49	482.25
15,500	485.71	487.50	489.30	491.09	492.90	494.70	496.51	498.32
16,000	501.38	503.23	505.08	506.94	508.80	510.66	512.53	514.40
16,500	517.05	518.96	520.86	522.78	524.70	526.62	528.54	530.47
17,000	532.72	534.68	536.65	538.62	540.60	542.58	544.56	546.55
17,500	548.39	550.41	552.43	554.46	556.50	558.53	560.58	562.62
18,000	564.05	566.13	568.22	570.30	572.40	574.49	576.59	578.70
18,500	579.72	581.86	584.00	586.14	588.30	590.45	592.61	594.77
19,000	595.39	597.58	599.78	601.99	604.19	606.41	608.63	610.85
19,500	611.06	613.31	615.57	617.83	620.09	622.37	624.64	626.92

Loan Amt.	8.00%	8.25%	8.50%	8.75%	9.00%	9.25%	9.50%	9.75%
20,000	626.73	629.04	631.35	633.67	635.99	638.32	640.66	643.00
20,500	642.40	644.76	647.13	649.51	651.89	654.28	656.68	659.07
21,000	658.06	660.49	662.92	665.35	667.79	670.24	672.69	675.15
21,500	673.73	676.21	678.70	681.20	683.69	686.20	688.71	691.22
22,000	689.40	691.94	694.49	697.04	699.59	702.16	704.72	707.30
22,500	705.07	707.67	710.27	712.88	715.49	718.11	720.74	723.37
23,000	720.74	723.39	726.05	728.72	731.39	734.07	736.76	739.45
23,500	736.40	739.12	741.84	744.56	747.29	750.03	752.77	755.52
24,000	752.07	754.84	757.62	760.40	763.19	765.99	768.79	771.60
24,500	767.74	770.57	773.40	776.25	779.09	781.95	784.81	787.67
25,000	783.41	786.30	789.19	792.09	794.99	797.91	800.82	803.75
25,500	799.08	802.02	804.97	807.93	810.89	813.86	816.84	819.82
26,000	814.75	817.75	820.76	823.77	826.79	829.82	832.86	835.90
26,500	830.41	833.47	836.54	839.61	842.69	845.78	848.87	851.97
27,000	846.08	849.20	852.32	855.45	858.59	861.74	864.89	868.05
27,500	861.75	864.93	868.11	871.30	874.49	877.70	880.91	884.12
28,000	877.42	880.65	883.89	887.14	890.39	893.65	896.92	900.20
28,500	893.09	896.38	899.67	902.98	906.29	909.61	912.94	916.27
29,000	908.75	912.10	915.46	918.82	922.19	925.57	928.96	932.35
29,500	924.42	927.83	931.24	934.66	938.09	941.53	944.97	948.42
30,000	940.09	943.55	947.03	950.51	953.99	957.49	960.99	964.50
30,500	955.76	959.28	962.81	966.35	969.89	973.44	977.00	980.57
31,000	971.43	975.01	978.59	982.19	985.79	989.40	993.02	996.65
31,500	987.10	990.73	994.38	998.03	1,001.69	1,005.36	1,009.04	1,012.72
32,000	1,002.76	1,006.46	1,010.16	1,013.87	1,017.59	1,021.32	1,025.05	1,028.80
32,500	1,018.43	1,022.18	1,025.94	1,029.71	1,033.49	1,037.28	1,041.07	1,044.87
33,000	1,034.10	1,037.91	1,041.73	1,045.56	1,049.39	1,053.24	1,057.09	1,060.95
33,500	1,049.77	1,053.64	1,057.51	1,061.40	1,065.29	1,069.19	1,073.10	1,077.02
34,000	1,065.44	1,069.36	1,073.30	1,077.24	1,081.19	1,085.15	1,089.12	1,093.10
34,500	1,081.10	1,085.09	1,089.08	1,093.08	1,097.09	1,101.11	1,105.14	1,109.17
35,000	1,096.77	1,100.81	1,104.86	1,108.92	1,112.99	1,117.07	1,121.15	1,125.25

MONTHLY PAYMENTS FOR 36-MONTH CONVENTIONAL LOANS (*continued*)

Loan Amt.	10.00%	10.25%	10.50%	10.75%	11.00%	11.25%	11.50%	11.75%
$ 500	16.13	16.19	16.25	16.31	16.37	16.43	16.49	16.55
1,000	32.27	32.38	32.50	32.62	32.74	32.86	32.98	33.10
1,500	48.40	48.58	48.75	48.93	49.11	49.29	49.46	49.64
2,000	64.53	64.77	65.00	65.24	65.48	65.71	65.95	66.19
2,500	80.67	80.96	81.26	81.55	81.85	82.14	82.44	82.74
3,000	96.80	97.15	97.51	97.86	98.22	98.57	98.93	99.29
3,500	112.94	113.35	113.76	114.17	114.59	115.00	115.42	115.83
4,000	129.07	129.54	130.01	130.48	130.95	131.43	131.90	132.38
4,500	145.20	145.73	146.26	146.79	147.32	147.86	148.39	148.93
5,000	161.34	161.92	162.51	163.10	163.69	164.29	164.88	165.48
5,500	177.47	178.12	178.76	179.41	180.06	180.71	181.37	182.02
6,000	193.60	194.31	195.01	195.72	196.43	197.14	197.86	198.57
6,500	209.74	210.50	211.27	212.03	212.80	213.57	214.34	215.12
7,000	225.87	226.69	227.52	228.34	229.17	230.00	230.83	231.67
7,500	242.00	242.89	243.77	244.65	245.54	246.43	247.32	248.21
8,000	258.14	259.08	260.02	260.96	261.91	262.86	263.81	264.76
8,500	274.27	275.27	276.27	277.27	278.28	279.29	280.30	281.31
9,000	290.40	291.46	292.52	293.58	294.65	295.72	296.78	297.86
9,500	306.54	307.65	308.77	309.89	311.02	312.14	313.27	314.40
10,000	322.67	323.85	325.02	326.20	327.39	328.57	329.76	330.95
10,500	338.81	340.04	341.28	342.51	343.76	345.00	346.25	347.50
11,000	354.94	356.23	357.53	358.82	360.13	361.43	362.74	364.05
11,500	371.07	372.42	373.78	375.14	376.50	377.86	379.22	380.59
12,000	387.21	388.62	390.03	391.45	392.86	394.29	395.71	397.14
12,500	403.34	404.81	406.28	407.76	409.23	410.72	412.20	413.69
13,000	419.47	421.00	422.53	424.07	425.60	427.14	428.69	430.24
13,500	435.61	437.19	438.78	440.38	441.97	443.57	445.18	446.78
14,000	451.74	453.39	455.03	456.69	458.34	460.00	461.66	463.33
14,500	467.87	469.58	471.29	473.00	474.71	476.43	478.15	479.88
15,000	484.01	485.77	487.54	489.31	491.08	492.86	494.64	496.43
15,500	500.14	501.96	503.79	505.62	507.45	509.29	511.13	512.97
16,000	516.27	518.16	520.04	521.93	523.82	525.72	527.62	529.52
16,500	532.41	534.35	536.29	538.24	540.19	542.14	544.10	546.07
17,000	548.54	550.54	552.54	554.55	556.56	558.57	560.59	562.62
17,500	564.68	566.73	568.79	570.86	572.93	575.00	577.08	579.16
18,000	580.81	582.92	585.04	587.17	589.30	591.43	593.57	595.71
18,500	596.94	599.12	601.30	603.48	605.67	607.86	610.06	612.26
19,000	613.08	615.31	617.55	619.79	622.04	624.29	626.54	628.81
19,500	629.21	631.50	633.80	636.10	638.40	640.72	643.03	645.35

12.00%	12.25%	12.50%	12.75%	13.00%	13.25%	13.50%	13.75%
16.61	16.67	16.73	16.79	16.85	16.91	16.97	17.03
33.21	33.33	33.45	33.57	33.69	33.81	33.94	34.06
49.82	50.00	50.18	50.36	50.54	50.72	50.90	51.08
66.43	66.67	66.91	67.15	67.39	67.63	67.87	68.11
83.04	83.33	83.63	83.93	84.23	84.54	84.84	85.14
99.64	100.00	100.36	100.72	101.08	101.44	101.81	102.17
116.25	116.67	117.09	117.51	117.93	118.35	118.77	119.20
132.86	133.34	133.81	134.29	134.78	135.26	135.74	136.23
149.46	150.00	150.54	151.08	151.62	152.17	152.71	153.25
166.07	166.67	167.27	167.87	168.47	169.07	169.68	170.28
182.68	183.34	183.99	184.66	185.32	185.98	186.64	187.31
199.29	200.00	200.72	201.44	202.16	202.89	203.61	204.34
215.89	216.67	217.45	218.23	219.01	219.79	220.58	221.37
232.50	233.34	234.18	235.02	235.86	236.70	237.55	238.39
249.11	250.00	250.90	251.80	252.70	253.61	254.51	255.42
265.71	266.67	267.63	268.59	269.55	270.52	271.48	272.45
282.32	283.34	284.36	285.38	286.40	287.42	288.45	289.48
298.93	300.00	301.08	302.16	303.25	304.33	305.42	306.51
315.54	316.67	317.81	318.95	320.09	321.24	322.39	323.54
332.14	333.34	334.54	335.74	336.94	338.14	339.35	340.56
348.75	350.01	351.26	352.52	353.79	355.05	356.32	357.59
365.36	366.67	367.99	369.31	370.63	371.96	373.29	374.62
381.96	383.34	384.72	386.10	387.48	388.87	390.26	391.65
398.57	400.01	401.44	402.88	404.33	405.77	407.22	408.68
415.18	416.67	418.17	419.67	421.17	422.68	424.19	425.70
431.79	433.34	434.90	436.46	438.02	439.59	441.16	442.73
448.39	450.01	451.62	453.24	454.87	456.50	458.13	459.76
465.00	466.67	468.35	470.03	471.72	473.40	475.09	476.79
481.61	483.34	485.08	486.82	488.56	490.31	492.06	493.82
498.21	500.01	501.80	503.60	505.41	507.22	509.03	510.84
514.82	516.67	518.53	520.39	522.26	524.12	526.00	527.87
531.43	533.34	535.26	537.18	539.10	541.03	542.96	544.90
548.04	550.01	551.98	553.97	555.95	557.94	559.93	561.93
564.64	566.68	568.71	570.75	572.80	574.85	576.90	578.96
581.25	583.34	585.44	587.54	589.64	591.75	593.87	595.99
597.86	600.01	602.17	604.33	606.49	608.66	610.84	613.01
614.46	616.68	618.89	621.11	623.34	625.57	627.80	630.04
631.07	633.34	635.62	637.90	640.19	642.48	644.77	647.07
647.68	650.01	652.35	654.69	657.03	659.38	661.74	664.10

MONTHLY PAYMENTS FOR 36-MONTH CONVENTIONAL LOANS (*continued*)

Loan Amt.	10.00%	10.25%	10.50%	10.75%	11.00%	11.25%	11.50%	11.75%
20,000	645.34	647.69	650.05	652.41	654.77	657.14	659.52	661.90
20,500	661.48	663.89	666.30	668.72	671.14	673.57	676.01	678.45
21,000	677.61	680.08	682.55	685.03	687.51	690.00	692.50	695.00
21,500	693.74	696.27	698.80	701.34	703.88	706.43	708.98	711.54
22,000	709.88	712.46	715.05	717.65	720.25	722.86	725.47	728.09
22,500	726.01	728.66	731.30	733.96	736.62	739.29	741.96	744.64
23,000	742.15	744.85	747.56	750.27	752.99	755.72	758.45	761.19
23,500	758.28	761.04	763.81	766.58	769.36	772.15	774.94	777.73
24,000	774.41	777.23	780.06	782.89	785.73	788.57	791.42	794.28
24,500	790.55	793.42	796.31	799.20	802.10	805.00	807.91	810.83
25,000	806.68	809.62	812.56	815.51	818.47	821.43	824.40	827.38
25,500	822.81	825.81	828.81	831.82	834.84	837.86	840.89	843.92
26,000	838.95	842.00	845.06	848.13	851.21	854.29	857.38	860.47
26,500	855.08	858.19	861.31	864.44	867.58	870.72	873.86	877.02
27,000	871.21	874.39	877.57	880.75	883.95	887.15	890.35	893.57
27,500	887.35	890.58	893.82	897.06	900.31	903.57	906.84	910.11
28,000	903.48	906.77	910.07	913.37	916.68	920.00	923.33	926.66
28,500	919.61	922.96	926.32	929.68	933.05	936.43	939.82	943.21
29,000	935.75	939.16	942.57	945.99	949.42	952.86	956.30	959.76
29,500	951.88	955.35	958.82	962.30	965.79	969.29	972.79	976.30
30,000	968.02	971.54	975.07	978.61	982.16	985.72	989.28	992.85
30,500	984.15	987.73	991.32	994.92	998.53	1,002.15	1,005.77	1,009.40
31,000	1,000.28	1,003.93	1,007.58	1,011.23	1,014.90	1,018.57	1,022.26	1,025.95
31,500	1,016.42	1,020.12	1,023.83	1,027.54	1,031.27	1,035.00	1,038.74	1,042.49
32,000	1,032.55	1,036.31	1,040.08	1,043.85	1,047.64	1,051.43	1,055.23	1,059.04
32,500	1,048.68	1,052.50	1,056.33	1,060.16	1,064.01	1,067.86	1,071.72	1,075.59
33,000	1,064.82	1,068.69	1,072.58	1,076.47	1,080.38	1,084.29	1,088.21	1,092.14
33,500	1,080.95	1,084.89	1,088.83	1,092.79	1,096.75	1,100.72	1,104.70	1,108.68
34,000	1,097.08	1,101.08	1,105.08	1,109.10	1,113.12	1,117.15	1,121.18	1,125.23
34,500	1,113.22	1,117.27	1,121.33	1,125.41	1,129.49	1,133.57	1,137.67	1,141.78
35,000	1,129.35	1,133.46	1,137.59	1,141.72	1,145.86	1,150.00	1,154.16	1,158.33

12.00%	12.25%	12.50%	12.75%	13.00%	13.25%	13.50%	13.75%
664.29	666.68	669.07	671.47	673.88	676.29	678.71	681.13
680.89	683.34	685.80	688.26	690.73	693.20	695.67	698.15
697.50	700.01	702.53	705.05	707.57	710.10	712.64	715.18
714.11	716.68	719.25	721.83	724.42	727.01	729.61	732.21
730.71	733.34	735.98	738.62	741.27	743.92	746.58	749.24
747.32	750.01	752.71	755.41	758.11	760.83	763.54	766.27
763.93	766.68	769.43	772.19	774.96	777.73	780.51	783.30
780.54	783.35	786.16	788.98	791.81	794.64	797.48	800.32
797.14	800.01	802.89	805.77	808.65	811.55	814.45	817.35
813.75	816.68	819.61	822.55	825.50	828.46	831.41	834.38
830.36	833.35	836.34	839.34	842.35	845.36	848.38	851.41
846.96	850.01	853.07	856.13	859.20	862.27	865.35	868.44
863.57	866.68	869.79	872.92	876.04	879.18	882.32	885.46
880.18	883.35	886.52	889.70	892.89	896.08	899.29	902.49
896.79	900.01	903.25	906.49	909.74	912.99	916.25	919.52
913.39	916.68	919.97	923.28	926.58	929.90	933.22	936.55
930.00	933.35	936.70	940.06	943.43	946.81	950.19	953.58
946.61	950.01	953.43	956.85	960.28	963.71	967.16	970.61
963.21	966.68	970.16	973.64	977.12	980.62	984.12	987.63
979.82	983.35	986.88	990.42	993.97	997.53	1,001.09	1,004.66
996.43	1,000.02	1,003.61	1,007.21	1,010.82	1,014.43	1,018.06	1,021.69
1,013.04	1,016.68	1,020.34	1,024.00	1,027.67	1,031.34	1,035.03	1,038.72
1,029.64	1,033.35	1,037.06	1,040.78	1,044.51	1,048.25	1,051.99	1,055.75
1,046.25	1,050.02	1,053.79	1,057.57	1,061.36	1,065.16	1,068.96	1,072.77
1,062.86	1,066.68	1,070.52	1,074.36	1,078.21	1,082.06	1,085.93	1,089.80
1,079.47	1,083.35	1,087.24	1,091.14	1,095.05	1,098.97	1,102.90	1,106.83
1,096.07	1,100.02	1,103.97	1,107.93	1,111.90	1,115.88	1,119.86	1,123.86
1,112.68	1,116.68	1,120.70	1,124.72	1,128.75	1,132.79	1,136.83	1,140.89
1,129.29	1,133.35	1,137.42	1,141.50	1,145.59	1,149.69	1,153.80	1,157.92
1,145.89	1,150.02	1,154.15	1,158.29	1,162.44	1,166.60	1,170.77	1,174.94
1,162.50	1,166.68	1,170.88	1,175.08	1,179.29	1,183.51	1,187.74	1,191.97

MONTHLY PAYMENTS FOR 48-MONTH CONVENTIONAL LOANS

Loan Amt.	8.00%	8.25%	8.50%	8.75%	9.00%	9.25%	9.50%	9.75%
$ 500	12.21	12.27	12.32	12.38	12.44	12.50	12.56	12.62
1,000	24.41	24.53	24.65	24.77	24.89	25.00	25.12	25.24
1,500	36.62	36.80	36.97	37.15	37.33	37.51	37.68	37.86
2,000	48.83	49.06	49.30	49.53	49.77	50.01	50.25	50.49
2,500	61.03	61.33	61.62	61.92	62.21	62.51	62.81	63.11
3,000	73.24	73.59	73.94	74.30	74.66	75.01	75.37	75.73
3,500	85.45	85.86	86.27	86.68	87.10	87.51	87.93	88.35
4,000	97.65	98.12	98.59	99.07	99.54	100.02	100.49	100.97
4,500	109.86	110.39	110.92	111.45	111.98	112.52	113.05	113.59
5,000	122.06	122.65	123.24	123.83	124.43	125.02	125.62	126.21
5,500	134.27	134.92	135.57	136.22	136.87	137.52	138.18	138.83
6,000	146.43	147.18	147.89	148.60	149.31	150.02	150.74	151.46
6,500	158.63	159.45	160.21	160.98	161.75	162.53	163.30	164.08
7,000	170.89	171.71	172.54	173.37	174.20	175.03	175.86	176.70
7,500	183.10	183.98	184.86	185.75	186.64	187.53	188.42	189.32
8,000	195.30	196.24	197.19	198.13	199.08	200.03	200.99	201.94
8,500	207.51	208.51	209.51	210.52	211.52	212.53	213.55	214.56
9,000	219.72	220.77	221.83	222.90	223.97	225.04	226.11	227.18
9,500	231.92	233.04	234.16	235.28	236.41	237.54	238.67	239.81
10,000	244.13	245.30	246.48	247.67	248.85	250.04	251.23	252.43
10,500	256.34	257.57	258.81	260.05	261.29	262.54	263.79	265.05
11,000	268.54	269.83	271.13	272.43	273.74	275.04	276.35	277.67
11,500	280.75	282.10	283.46	284.81	286.18	287.55	288.92	290.29
12,000	292.98	294.37	295.78	297.20	298.62	300.05	301.48	302.91
12,500	305.15	306.63	308.10	309.58	311.06	312.55	314.04	315.53
13,000	317.37	318.90	320.43	321.96	323.51	325.05	326.60	328.15
13,500	329.57	331.16	332.75	334.35	335.95	337.55	339.16	340.78
14,000	341.73	343.43	345.08	346.73	348.39	350.05	351.72	353.40
14,500	353.99	355.69	357.40	359.11	360.83	362.56	364.29	366.02
15,000	366.19	367.96	369.72	371.50	373.28	375.06	376.85	378.64
15,500	378.40	380.22	382.05	383.88	385.72	387.56	389.41	391.26
16,000	390.61	392.49	394.37	396.26	398.16	400.06	401.97	403.88
16,500	402.81	404.75	406.70	408.65	410.60	412.56	414.53	416.50
17,000	415.02	417.02	419.02	421.03	423.05	425.07	427.09	429.13
17,500	427.23	429.28	431.35	433.41	435.49	437.57	439.65	441.75
18,000	439.43	441.55	443.67	445.80	447.93	450.07	452.22	454.37
18,500	451.64	453.81	455.99	458.18	460.37	462.57	464.78	466.99
19,000	463.85	466.08	468.32	470.56	472.82	475.07	477.34	479.61
19,500	476.05	478.34	480.64	482.95	485.26	487.58	489.90	492.23

10.00%	10.25%	10.50%	10.75%	11.00%	11.25%	11.50%	11.75%
12.68	12.74	12.80	12.86	12.92	12.98	13.04	13.11
25.36	25.48	25.60	25.72	25.85	25.97	26.09	26.21
38.04	38.22	38.41	38.59	38.77	38.95	39.13	39.32
50.73	50.97	51.21	51.45	51.69	51.93	52.18	52.42
63.41	63.71	64.01	64.31	64.61	64.92	65.22	65.53
76.09	76.45	76.81	77.17	77.54	77.90	78.27	78.63
88.77	89.19	89.61	90.03	90.46	90.88	91.31	91.74
101.45	101.93	102.41	102.90	103.38	103.87	104.36	104.85
114.13	114.67	115.22	115.76	116.30	116.85	117.40	117.95
126.81	127.41	128.02	128.62	129.23	129.84	130.45	131.06
139.49	140.16	140.82	141.48	142.15	142.82	143.49	144.16
152.18	152.90	153.62	154.35	155.07	155.80	156.53	157.27
164.86	165.64	166.42	167.21	168.00	168.79	169.58	170.37
177.54	178.38	179.22	180.07	180.92	181.77	182.62	183.48
190.22	191.12	192.03	192.93	193.84	194.75	195.67	196.58
202.90	203.86	204.83	205.79	206.76	207.74	208.71	209.69
215.58	216.60	217.63	218.66	219.69	220.72	221.76	222.80
228.26	229.35	230.43	231.52	232.61	233.70	234.80	235.90
240.94	242.09	243.23	244.38	245.53	246.69	247.85	249.01
253.63	254.83	256.03	257.24	258.46	259.67	260.89	262.11
266.31	267.57	268.84	270.10	271.38	272.65	273.93	275.22
278.99	280.31	281.64	282.97	284.30	285.64	286.98	288.32
291.67	293.05	294.44	295.83	297.22	298.62	300.02	301.43
304.35	305.79	307.24	308.69	310.15	311.61	313.07	314.54
317.03	318.54	320.04	321.55	323.07	324.59	326.11	327.64
329.71	331.28	332.84	334.42	335.99	337.57	339.16	340.75
342.39	344.02	345.65	347.28	348.91	350.56	352.20	353.85
355.08	356.76	358.45	360.14	361.84	363.54	365.25	366.96
367.76	369.50	371.25	373.00	374.76	376.52	378.29	380.06
380.44	382.24	384.05	385.86	387.68	389.51	391.34	393.17
393.12	394.98	396.85	398.73	400.61	402.49	404.38	406.27
405.80	407.73	409.65	411.59	413.53	415.47	417.42	419.38
418.48	420.47	422.46	424.45	426.45	428.46	430.47	432.49
431.16	433.21	435.26	437.31	439.37	441.44	443.51	445.59
443.85	445.95	448.06	450.17	452.30	454.42	456.56	458.70
456.53	458.69	460.86	463.04	465.22	467.41	469.60	471.80
469.21	471.43	473.66	475.90	478.14	480.39	482.65	484.91
481.89	484.17	486.46	488.76	491.06	493.37	495.69	498.01
494.57	496.91	499.27	501.62	503.99	506.36	508.74	511.12

MONTHLY PAYMENTS FOR 48-MONTH CONVENTIONAL LOANS (*continued*)

Loan Amt.	8.00%	8.25%	8.50%	8.75%	9.00%	9.25%	9.50%	9.75%
20,000	488.25	490.61	492.97	495.33	497.70	500.08	502.46	504.85
20,500	500.46	502.87	505.29	507.71	510.14	512.58	515.02	517.48
21,000	512.67	515.14	517.61	520.10	522.59	525.08	527.59	530.10
21,500	524.88	527.40	529.94	532.48	535.03	537.58	540.15	542.72
22,000	537.08	539.67	542.26	544.86	547.47	550.09	552.71	555.34
22,500	549.29	551.93	554.59	557.25	559.91	562.59	565.27	567.96
23,000	561.50	564.20	566.91	569.63	572.36	575.09	577.83	580.58
23,500	573.70	576.47	579.24	582.01	584.80	587.59	590.39	593.20
24,000	585.91	588.73	591.56	594.40	597.24	600.09	602.96	605.82
24,500	598.12	601.00	603.88	606.78	609.68	612.60	615.52	618.45
25,000	610.32	613.26	616.21	619.16	622.13	625.10	628.08	631.07
25,500	622.53	625.53	628.53	631.55	634.57	637.60	640.64	643.69
26,000	634.74	637.79	640.86	643.93	647.01	650.10	653.20	656.31
26,500	646.94	650.06	653.18	656.31	659.45	662.60	665.76	668.93
27,000	659.15	662.32	665.50	668.70	671.90	675.11	678.32	681.55
27,500	671.35	674.59	677.83	681.08	684.34	687.61	690.89	694.17
28,000	683.55	686.85	690.15	693.46	696.78	700.11	703.45	706.80
28,500	695.77	699.12	702.48	705.85	709.22	712.61	716.01	719.42
29,000	707.97	711.38	714.80	718.23	721.67	725.11	728.57	732.04
29,500	720.18	723.65	727.12	730.61	734.11	737.62	741.13	744.66
30,000	732.39	735.91	739.45	743.00	746.55	750.12	753.69	757.28
30,500	744.59	748.18	751.77	755.38	758.99	762.62	766.26	769.90
31,000	756.80	760.44	764.10	767.76	771.44	775.12	778.82	782.52
31,500	769.01	772.71	776.42	780.14	783.88	787.62	791.38	795.14
32,000	781.21	784.97	788.75	792.53	796.32	800.13	803.94	807.77
32,500	793.42	797.24	801.07	804.91	808.76	812.63	816.50	820.39
33,000	805.63	809.50	813.39	817.29	821.21	825.13	829.06	833.01
33,500	817.83	821.77	825.72	829.68	833.65	837.63	841.63	845.63
34,000	830.04	834.04	838.04	842.06	846.09	850.13	854.19	858.25
34,500	842.25	846.30	850.37	854.44	858.53	862.64	866.75	870.87
35,000	854.45	858.57	862.69	866.83	870.98	875.14	879.31	883.49

10.00%	10.25%	10.50%	10.75%	11.00%	11.25%	11.50%	11.75%
507.25	509.66	512.07	514.49	516.91	519.34	521.78	524.23
519.93	522.40	524.87	527.35	529.83	532.33	534.82	537.33
532.61	535.14	537.67	540.21	542.76	545.31	547.87	550.44
545.30	547.88	550.47	553.07	555.68	558.29	560.91	563.54
557.98	560.62	563.27	565.93	568.60	571.28	573.96	576.65
570.66	573.36	576.08	578.80	581.52	584.26	587.00	589.75
583.34	586.10	588.88	591.66	594.45	597.24	600.05	602.86
596.02	598.85	601.68	604.52	607.37	610.23	613.09	615.96
608.70	611.59	614.48	617.38	620.29	623.21	626.14	629.07
621.38	624.33	627.28	630.24	633.22	636.19	639.18	642.18
634.06	637.07	640.08	643.11	646.14	649.18	652.23	655.28
646.75	649.81	652.89	655.97	659.06	662.16	665.27	668.39
659.43	662.55	665.69	668.83	671.98	675.14	678.31	681.49
672.11	675.29	678.49	681.69	684.91	688.13	691.36	694.60
684.79	688.04	691.29	694.56	697.83	701.11	704.40	707.70
697.47	700.78	704.09	707.42	710.75	714.10	717.45	720.81
710.15	713.52	716.89	720.28	723.67	727.08	730.49	733.92
722.83	726.26	729.70	733.14	736.60	740.06	743.54	747.02
735.51	739.00	742.50	746.00	749.52	753.05	756.58	760.13
748.20	751.74	755.30	758.87	762.44	766.03	769.63	773.23
760.88	764.48	768.10	771.73	775.37	779.01	782.67	786.34
773.56	777.23	780.90	784.59	788.29	792.00	795.71	799.44
786.24	789.97	793.70	797.45	801.21	804.98	808.76	812.55
798.92	802.71	806.51	810.31	814.13	817.96	821.80	825.65
811.60	815.45	819.31	823.18	827.06	830.95	834.85	838.76
824.28	828.19	832.11	836.04	839.98	843.93	847.89	851.87
836.97	840.93	844.91	848.90	852.90	856.91	860.94	864.97
849.65	853.67	857.71	861.76	865.83	869.90	873.98	878.08
862.33	866.42	870.51	874.63	878.75	882.88	887.03	891.18
875.01	879.16	883.32	887.49	891.67	895.86	900.07	904.29
887.69	891.90	896.12	900.35	904.59	908.85	913.12	917.39

MONTHLY PAYMENTS FOR 48-MONTH
CONVENTIONAL LOANS (*continued*)

Loan Amt.	12.00%	12.25%	12.50%	12.75%	13.00%	13.25%	13.50%	13.75%
$ 500	13.17	13.23	13.29	13.35	13.41	13.48	13.54	13.60
1,000	26.33	26.46	26.58	26.70	26.83	26.95	27.08	27.20
1,500	39.50	39.69	39.87	40.06	40.24	40.43	40.61	40.80
2,000	52.67	52.91	53.16	53.41	53.65	53.90	54.15	54.40
2,500	65.83	66.14	66.45	66.76	67.07	67.38	67.69	68.00
3,000	79.00	79.37	79.74	80.11	80.48	80.86	81.23	81.60
3,500	92.17	92.60	93.03	93.46	93.90	94.33	94.77	95.20
4,000	105.34	105.83	106.32	106.81	107.31	107.81	108.31	108.80
4,500	118.50	119.06	119.61	120.17	120.72	121.28	121.84	122.41
5,000	131.67	132.28	132.90	133.52	134.14	134.76	135.38	136.01
5,500	144.84	145.51	146.19	146.87	147.55	148.23	148.92	149.61
6,000	158.00	158.74	159.48	160.22	160.96	161.71	162.46	163.21
6,500	171.17	171.97	172.77	173.57	174.38	175.19	176.00	176.81
7,000	164.34	185.20	186.06	186.93	187.79	188.66	189.53	190.41
7,500	197.50	198.43	199.35	200.28	201.21	202.14	203.07	204.01
8,000	210.67	211.65	212.64	213.63	214.62	215.61	216.61	217.61
8,500	223.84	224.88	225.93	226.98	228.03	229.09	230.15	231.21
9,000	237.00	238.11	239.22	240.33	241.45	242.57	243.69	244.81
9,500	250.17	251.34	252.51	253.68	254.86	256.04	257.23	258.41
10,000	263.34	264.57	265.80	267.04	268.27	269.52	270.76	272.01
10,500	276.51	277.80	279.09	280.39	281.69	282.99	284.30	285.61
11,000	289.67	291.02	292.38	293.74	295.10	296.47	297.84	299.21
11,500	302.84	304.25	305.67	307.90	308.52	309.95	311.38	312.81
12,000	316.01	317.48	318.96	320.44	321.93	323.42	324.92	326.41
12,500	329.17	330.71	332.25	333.79	335.34	336.90	338.45	340.02
13,000	342.34	343.94	345.54	347.15	348.76	350.37	351.99	353.62
13,500	355.51	357.17	358.83	360.50	362.17	363.85	365.53	367.22
14,000	368.67	370.39	372.12	373.85	375.58	377.32	379.07	380.82
14,500	381.84	383.62	385.41	387.20	389.00	390.80	392.61	394.42
15,000	395.01	396.85	398.70	400.55	402.41	404.28	406.14	408.02
15,500	408.17	410.08	411.99	413.91	415.83	417.75	419.68	421.62
16,000	421.34	423.31	425.28	427.26	429.24	431.23	433.22	435.22
16,500	434.51	436.54	438.57	440.61	442.65	444.70	446.76	448.82
17,000	447.68	449.76	451.86	453.96	456.07	458.18	460.30	462.42
17,500	460.84	462.99	465.15	467.31	469.48	471.66	473.84	476.02
18,000	474.01	476.22	478.44	480.66	482.89	485.13	487.37	489.62
18,500	487.18	489.45	491.73	494.02	496.31	498.61	500.91	503.22
19,000	500.34	502.68	505.02	507.37	509.72	512.08	514.45	516.82
19,500	513.51	515.91	518.31	520.72	523.14	525.56	527.99	530.42

Loan Amt.	12.00%	12.25%	12.50%	12.75%	13.00%	13.25%	13.50%	13.75%
20,000	526.68	529.14	531.60	534.07	536.55	539.03	541.53	544.02
20,500	539.84	542.36	544.89	547.42	549.96	552.51	555.06	557.63
21,000	553.01	555.59	558.18	560.78	563.38	565.99	568.60	571.23
21,500	566.18	568.82	571.47	574.13	576.79	579.46	582.14	584.83
22,000	579.34	582.05	584.76	587.48	590.20	592.94	595.68	598.43
22,500	592.51	595.28	598.05	600.83	603.62	606.41	609.22	612.03
23,000	605.68	608.51	611.34	614.18	617.03	619.89	622.76	625.63
23,500	618.85	621.73	624.63	627.53	630.45	633.37	636.29	639.23
24,000	632.01	634.96	637.92	640.89	643.86	646.84	649.83	652.83
24,500	645.18	648.19	651.21	654.24	657.27	660.32	663.37	666.43
25,000	658.35	661.42	664.50	667.59	670.69	673.79	676.91	680.03
25,500	671.51	674.65	677.79	680.94	684.10	687.27	690.45	693.63
26,000	684.68	687.88	691.08	694.29	697.51	700.75	703.98	707.23
26,500	697.85	701.10	704.37	707.64	710.93	714.22	717.52	720.83
27,000	711.01	714.33	717.66	721.00	724.34	727.70	731.06	734.43
27,500	724.18	727.56	730.95	734.35	737.76	741.17	744.60	748.03
28,000	737.35	740.79	744.24	747.70	751.17	754.65	758.14	761.63
28,500	750.51	754.02	757.53	761.05	764.58	768.12	771.68	775.24
29,000	763.68	767.25	770.82	774.40	778.00	781.60	785.21	788.84
29,500	776.85	780.47	784.11	787.76	791.41	795.08	798.75	802.44
30,000	790.02	793.70	797.40	801.11	804.82	808.55	812.29	816.04
30,500	803.18	806.93	810.69	814.46	818.24	822.03	825.83	829.64
31,000	816.35	820.16	823.98	827.81	831.65	835.50	839.37	843.24
31,500	829.52	833.39	837.27	841.16	845.07	848.98	852.90	856.84
32,000	842.68	846.62	850.56	854.51	858.48	862.46	866.44	870.44
32,500	855.85	859.84	863.85	867.87	871.89	875.93	879.98	884.04
33,000	869.02	873.07	877.14	881.22	885.31	889.41	893.52	897.64
33,500	882.18	886.30	890.43	894.57	898.72	902.88	907.06	911.24
34,000	895.35	899.53	903.72	907.92	912.13	916.36	920.59	924.84
34,500	908.52	912.76	917.01	921.27	925.55	929.84	934.13	938.44
35,000	921.68	925.99	930.30	934.63	938.96	943.31	947.67	952.04

MONTHLY PAYMENTS FOR 60-MONTH CONVENTIONAL LOANS

Loan Amt.	8.00%	8.25%	8.50%	8.75%	9.00%	9.25%	9.50%	9.75%
$ 500	10.14	10.20	10.26	10.32	10.38	10.44	10.50	10.56
1,000	20.28	20.40	20.52	20.64	20.76	20.88	21.00	21.12
1,500	30.41	30.59	30.77	30.96	31.14	31.32	31.50	31.69
2,000	40.55	40.79	41.03	41.27	41.52	41.76	42.00	42.25
2,500	50.69	50.99	51.29	51.59	51.90	52.20	52.50	52.81
3,000	60.83	61.19	61.55	61.91	62.28	62.64	63.01	63.37
3,500	70.97	71.39	71.81	72.23	72.65	73.08	73.51	73.93
4,000	81.11	81.59	82.07	82.55	83.03	83.52	84.01	84.50
4,500	91.24	91.78	92.32	92.87	93.41	93.96	94.51	95.06
5,000	101.38	101.98	102.58	103.19	103.79	104.40	105.01	105.62
5,500	111.52	112.18	112.84	113.50	114.17	114.84	115.51	116.18
6,000	121.66	122.38	123.10	123.82	124.55	125.28	126.01	126.75
6,500	131.80	132.58	133.36	134.14	134.93	135.72	136.51	137.31
7,000	141.93	142.77	143.62	144.46	145.31	146.16	147.01	147.87
7,500	152.07	152.97	153.87	154.78	155.69	156.60	157.51	158.43
8,000	162.21	163.17	164.13	165.10	166.07	167.04	168.01	168.99
8,500	172.35	173.37	174.39	175.42	176.45	177.48	178.52	179.56
9,000	182.49	183.57	184.65	185.74	186.83	187.92	189.02	190.12
9,500	192.63	193.76	194.91	196.05	197.20	198.36	199.52	200.68
10,000	202.76	203.96	205.17	206.37	207.58	208.80	210.02	211.24
10,500	212.90	214.16	215.42	216.69	217.96	219.24	220.52	221.80
11,000	223.04	224.36	225.68	227.01	228.34	229.68	231.02	232.37
11,500	233.18	234.56	235.94	237.33	238.72	240.12	241.52	242.93
12,000	243.32	244.76	246.20	247.65	249.10	250.56	252.02	253.49
12,500	253.45	254.95	256.46	257.97	259.48	261.00	262.52	264.05
13,000	263.59	265.15	266.71	268.28	269.86	271.44	273.02	274.62
13,500	273.73	275.35	276.97	278.60	280.24	281.88	283.53	285.18
14,000	283.87	285.55	287.23	288.92	290.62	292.32	294.03	295.74
14,500	294.01	295.75	297.49	299.24	301.00	302.76	304.53	306.30
15,000	304.15	305.94	307.75	309.56	311.38	313.20	315.03	316.86
15,500	314.28	316.14	318.01	319.88	321.75	323.64	325.53	327.43
16,000	324.42	326.34	328.26	330.20	332.13	334.08	336.03	337.99
16,500	334.56	336.54	338.52	340.51	342.51	344.52	346.53	348.55
17,000	344.70	346.74	348.78	350.83	352.89	354.96	357.03	359.11
17,500	354.84	356.93	359.04	361.15	363.27	365.40	367.53	369.67
18,000	364.98	367.13	369.30	371.47	373.65	375.84	378.03	380.24
18,500	375.11	377.33	379.56	381.79	384.03	386.28	388.53	390.80
19,000	385.25	387.53	389.81	392.11	394.41	396.72	399.04	401.36
19,500	395.39	397.73	400.07	402.43	404.79	407.16	409.54	411.92

Loan Amt.	8.00%	8.25%	8.50%	8.75%	9.00%	9.25%	9.50%	9.75%
20,000	405.53	407.93	410.33	412.74	415.17	417.60	420.04	422.48
20,500	415.67	418.12	420.59	423.06	425.55	428.04	430.54	433.05
21,000	425.80	428.32	430.85	433.38	435.93	438.48	441.04	443.61
21,500	435.94	438.52	441.11	443.70	446.30	448.92	451.54	454.17
22,000	446.08	448.72	451.36	454.02	456.68	459.36	462.04	464.73
22,500	456.22	458.92	461.62	464.34	467.06	469.80	472.54	475.30
23,000	466.36	469.11	471.88	474.66	477.44	480.24	483.04	485.86
23,500	476.50	479.31	482.14	484.97	487.82	490.68	493.54	496.42
24,000	486.63	489.51	492.40	495.29	498.20	501.12	504.04	506.98
24,500	496.77	499.71	502.66	505.61	508.58	511.56	514.55	517.54
25,000	506.91	509.91	512.91	515.93	518.96	522.00	525.05	528.11
25,500	517.05	520.10	523.17	526.25	529.34	532.44	535.55	538.67
26,000	527.19	530.30	533.43	536.57	539.72	542.88	546.05	549.23
26,500	537.32	540.50	543.69	546.89	550.10	553.32	556.55	559.79
27,000	547.46	550.70	553.95	557.21	560.48	563.76	567.05	570.35
27,500	557.60	560.90	564.20	567.52	570.85	574.20	577.55	580.92
28,000	567.74	571.10	574.46	577.84	581.23	584.64	588.05	591.48
28,500	577.88	581.29	584.72	588.16	591.61	595.08	598.55	602.04
29,000	588.02	591.49	594.98	598.48	601.99	605.52	609.05	612.60
29,500	598.15	601.69	605.24	608.80	612.37	615.96	619.55	623.17
30,000	608.29	611.89	615.50	619.12	622.75	626.40	630.06	633.73
30,500	618.43	622.09	625.75	629.44	633.13	636.84	640.56	644.29
31,000	628.57	632.28	636.01	639.75	643.51	647.28	651.06	654.85
31,500	638.71	642.48	646.27	650.07	653.89	657.72	661.56	665.41
32,000	648.84	652.68	656.53	660.39	664.27	668.16	672.06	675.98
32,500	658.98	662.88	666.79	670.71	674.65	678.60	682.56	686.54
33,000	669.12	673.08	677.05	681.03	685.03	689.04	693.06	697.10
33,500	679.26	683.27	687.30	691.35	695.40	699.48	703.56	707.66
34,000	689.40	693.47	697.56	701.67	705.78	709.92	714.06	718.22
34,500	699.54	703.67	707.82	711.98	716.16	720.36	724.56	728.79
35,000	709.67	713.87	718.08	722.30	726.54	730.80	735.07	739.35

Monthly Payments for 60-Month Conventional Loans (*continued*)

Loan Amt.	10.00%	10.25%	10.50%	10.75%	11.00%	11.25%	11.50%	11.75%
$ 500	10.62	10.69	10.75	10.81	10.87	10.93	11.00	11.06
1,000	21.25	21.37	21.49	21.62	21.74	21.87	21.99	22.12
1,500	31.87	32.06	32.24	32.43	32.61	32.80	32.99	33.18
2,000	42.49	42.74	42.99	43.24	43.48	43.73	43.99	44.24
2,500	53.12	53.43	53.73	54.04	54.36	54.67	54.98	55.30
3,000	63.74	64.11	64.48	64.85	65.23	65.60	65.98	66.35
3,500	74.36	74.80	75.23	75.66	76.10	76.54	76.97	77.41
4,000	84.99	85.48	85.98	86.47	86.97	87.47	87.97	88.47
4,500	95.61	96.17	96.72	97.28	97.84	98.40	98.97	99.53
5,000	106.24	106.85	107.47	108.09	108.71	109.34	109.96	110.59
5,500	116.86	117.54	118.22	118.90	119.58	120.27	120.96	121.65
6,000	127.48	128.22	128.96	129.71	130.45	131.20	131.96	132.71
6,500	138.11	138.91	139.71	140.52	141.33	142.14	142.95	143.77
7,000	148.73	149.59	150.46	151.33	152.20	153.07	153.95	154.83
7,500	159.35	160.28	161.20	162.13	163.07	164.00	164.94	165.89
8,000	169.98	170.96	171.95	172.94	173.94	174.94	175.94	176.95
8,500	180.60	181.65	182.70	183.75	184.81	185.87	186.94	188.01
9,000	191.22	192.33	193.45	194.56	195.68	196.81	197.93	199.06
9,500	201.85	203.02	204.19	205.37	206.55	207.74	208.93	210.12
10,000	212.47	213.70	214.94	216.18	217.42	218.67	219.93	221.18
10,500	223.09	224.39	225.69	226.99	228.30	229.61	230.92	232.24
11,000	233.72	235.07	236.43	237.80	239.17	240.54	241.92	243.30
11,500	244.34	245.76	247.18	248.61	250.04	251.47	252.91	254.36
12,000	254.96	256.44	257.93	259.42	260.91	262.41	263.91	265.42
12,500	265.59	267.13	268.67	270.22	271.78	273.34	274.91	276.48
13,000	276.21	277.81	279.42	281.03	282.65	284.28	285.90	287.54
13,500	286.84	288.50	290.17	291.84	293.52	295.21	296.90	298.60
14,000	297.46	299.18	300.91	302.65	304.39	306.14	307.90	309.66
14,500	308.08	309.87	311.66	313.46	315.27	317.08	318.89	320.72
15,000	318.71	320.55	322.41	324.27	326.14	328.01	329.89	331.77
15,500	329.33	331.24	333.16	335.08	337.01	338.94	340.89	342.83
16,000	339.95	341.92	343.90	345.89	347.88	349.88	351.88	353.89
16,500	350.58	352.61	354.65	356.70	358.75	360.81	362.88	364.95
17,000	361.20	363.29	365.40	367.51	369.62	371.74	373.87	376.01
17,500	371.82	373.98	376.14	378.31	380.49	382.68	384.87	387.07
18,000	382.45	384.66	386.89	389.12	391.36	393.61	395.87	398.13
18,500	393.07	395.35	397.64	399.93	402.23	404.55	406.86	409.19
19,000	403.69	406.04	408.38	410.74	413.11	415.48	417.86	420.25
19,500	414.32	416.72	419.13	421.55	423.98	426.41	428.86	431.31

12.00%	12.25%	12.50%	12.75%	13.00%	13.25%	13.50%	13.75%
11.12	11.19	11.25	11.31	11.38	11.44	11.50	11.57
22.24	22.37	22.50	22.63	22.75	22.88	23.01	23.14
33.37	33.56	33.75	33.94	34.13	34.32	34.51	34.71
44.49	44.74	45.00	45.25	45.51	45.76	46.02	46.28
55.61	55.93	56.24	56.56	56.88	57.20	57.52	57.85
66.73	67.11	67.49	67.88	68.26	68.64	69.03	69.42
77.86	78.30	78.74	79.19	79.64	80.08	80.53	80.99
88.98	89.48	89.99	90.50	91.01	91.53	92.04	92.56
100.10	100.67	101.24	101.81	102.39	102.97	103.54	104.12
111.22	111.85	112.49	113.13	113.77	114.41	115.05	115.69
122.34	123.04	123.74	124.44	125.14	125.85	126.55	127.26
133.47	134.23	134.99	135.75	136.52	137.29	138.06	138.83
144.59	145.41	146.24	147.06	147.89	148.73	149.56	150.40
155.71	156.60	157.49	158.38	159.27	160.17	161.07	161.97
166.83	167.78	168.73	169.69	170.65	171.61	172.57	173.54
177.96	178.97	179.98	181.00	182.02	183.05	184.08	185.11
189.08	190.15	191.23	192.32	193.40	194.49	195.58	196.68
200.20	201.34	202.48	203.63	204.78	205.93	207.09	208.25
211.32	212.52	213.73	214.94	216.15	217.37	218.59	219.82
222.44	223.71	224.98	226.25	227.53	228.81	230.10	231.39
233.57	234.90	236.23	237.57	238.91	240.25	241.60	242.96
244.69	246.08	247.48	248.88	250.28	251.69	253.11	254.53
255.81	257.27	258.73	260.19	261.66	263.13	264.61	266.10
266.93	268.45	269.98	271.50	273.04	274.58	276.12	277.67
278.06	279.64	281.22	282.82	284.41	286.02	287.62	289.24
289.18	290.82	292.47	294.13	295.79	297.46	299.13	300.80
300.30	302.01	303.72	305.44	307.17	308.90	310.63	312.37
311.42	313.19	314.97	316.75	318.54	320.34	322.14	323.94
322.54	324.38	326.22	328.07	329.92	331.78	333.64	335.51
333.67	335.56	337.47	339.38	341.30	343.22	345.15	347.08
344.79	346.75	348.72	350.69	352.57	354.66	356.65	358.65
355.91	357.94	359.97	362.00	364.05	366.10	368.16	370.22
367.03	369.12	371.22	373.32	375.43	377.54	379.66	381.79
378.16	380.31	382.46	384.63	386.80	388.98	391.17	393.36
389.28	391.49	393.71	395.94	398.18	400.42	402.67	404.93
400.40	402.68	404.96	407.26	409.56	411.86	414.18	416.50
411.52	413.86	416.21	418.57	420.93	423.30	425.68	428.07
422.64	425.05	427.46	429.88	432.31	434.74	437.19	439.64
433.77	436.23	438.71	441.19	443.68	446.18	448.69	451.21

MONTHLY PAYMENTS FOR 60-MONTH CONVENTIONAL LOANS (*continued*)

Loan Amt.	10.00%	10.25%	10.50%	10.75%	11.00%	11.25%	11.50%	11.75%
20,000	424.94	427.41	429.88	432.36	434.85	437.35	439.85	442.37
20,500	435.56	438.09	440.62	443.17	445.72	448.28	450.85	453.43
21,000	446.19	448.78	451.37	453.98	456.59	459.21	461.84	464.48
21,500	456.81	459.46	462.12	464.79	467.46	470.15	472.84	475.54
22,000	467.43	470.15	472.87	475.59	478.33	481.08	483.84	486.60
22,500	478.06	480.83	483.61	486.40	489.20	492.01	494.83	497.66
23,000	488.68	491.52	494.36	497.21	500.08	502.95	505.83	508.72
23,500	499.31	502.20	505.11	508.02	510.95	513.88	516.83	519.78
24,000	509.93	512.89	515.85	518.83	521.82	524.82	527.82	530.84
24,500	520.55	523.57	526.60	529.64	532.69	535.75	538.82	541.90
25,000	531.18	534.26	537.35	540.45	543.56	546.68	549.82	552.96
25,500	541.80	544.94	548.09	551.26	554.43	557.62	560.81	564.02
26,000	552.42	555.63	558.84	562.07	565.30	568.55	571.81	575.08
26,500	563.05	566.31	569.59	572.88	576.17	579.48	582.80	586.14
27,000	573.67	577.00	580.34	583.68	587.05	590.42	593.80	597.19
27,500	584.29	587.68	591.08	594.49	597.92	601.35	604.80	608.25
28,000	594.92	598.37	601.83	605.30	608.79	612.28	615.79	619.31
28,500	605.54	609.05	612.58	616.11	619.66	623.22	626.79	630.37
29,000	616.16	619.74	623.32	626.92	630.53	634.15	637.79	641.43
29,500	626.79	630.42	634.07	637.73	641.40	645.09	648.78	652.49
30,000	637.41	641.11	644.82	648.54	652.27	656.02	659.78	663.55
30,500	648.03	651.79	655.56	659.35	663.14	666.95	670.77	674.61
31,000	658.66	662.48	666.31	670.16	674.02	677.89	681.77	685.67
31,500	669.28	673.16	677.06	680.97	684.89	688.82	692.77	696.73
32,000	679.91	683.85	687.80	691.77	695.76	699.75	703.76	707.79
32,500	690.53	694.53	698.55	702.58	706.63	710.69	714.76	718.85
33,000	701.15	705.22	709.30	713.39	717.50	721.62	725.76	729.90
33,500	711.78	715.90	720.05	724.20	728.37	732.55	736.75	740.96
34,000	722.40	726.59	730.79	735.01	739.24	743.49	747.75	752.02
34,500	733.02	737.27	741.54	745.82	750.11	754.42	758.74	763.08
35,000	743.65	747.96	752.29	756.63	760.98	765.36	769.74	774.14

12.00%	12.25%	12.50%	12.75%	13.00%	13.25%	13.50%	13.75%
444.89	447.42	449.96	452.51	455.06	457.63	460.20	462.78
456.01	458.61	461.21	463.82	466.44	469.07	471.70	474.35
467.13	469.79	472.46	475.13	477.81	480.51	483.21	485.92
478.26	480.98	483.71	486.44	489.19	491.95	494.71	497.49
489.38	492.16	494.95	497.76	500.57	503.39	506.22	509.05
500.50	503.35	506.20	509.07	511.94	514.83	517.72	520.62
511.62	514.53	517.45	520.38	523.32	526.27	529.23	532.19
522.74	525.72	528.70	531.69	534.70	537.71	540.73	543.76
533.87	536.90	539.95	543.01	546.07	549.15	552.24	555.33
544.99	548.09	551.20	554.32	557.45	560.59	563.74	566.90
556.11	559.27	562.45	565.63	568.83	572.03	575.25	578.47
567.23	570.46	573.70	576.95	580.20	583.47	586.75	590.04
578.36	581.65	584.95	588.26	591.58	594.91	598.26	601.61
589.48	592.83	596.20	599.57	602.96	606.35	609.76	613.18
600.60	604.02	607.44	610.88	614.33	617.79	621.27	624.75
611.72	615.20	618.69	622.20	625.71	629.23	632.77	636.32
622.84	626.39	629.94	633.51	637.09	640.68	644.28	647.89
633.97	637.57	641.19	644.82	648.46	652.12	655.78	659.46
645.09	648.76	652.44	656.13	659.84	663.56	667.29	671.03
656.21	659.94	663.69	667.45	671.22	675.00	678.79	682.60
667.33	671.13	674.94	678.76	682.59	686.44	690.30	694.17
678.46	682.32	686.19	690.07	693.97	697.88	701.80	705.73
689.58	693.50	697.44	701.38	705.35	709.32	713.31	717.30
700.70	704.69	708.69	712.70	716.72	720.76	724.81	728.87
711.82	715.87	719.93	724.01	728.10	732.20	736.32	740.44
722.94	727.06	731.18	735.32	739.47	743.64	747.82	752.01
734.07	738.24	742.43	746.63	750.85	755.08	759.32	763.58
745.19	749.43	753.68	757.95	762.23	766.52	770.83	775.15
756.31	760.61	764.93	769.26	773.60	777.96	782.33	786.72
767.43	771.80	776.18	780.57	784.98	789.40	793.84	798.29
778.56	782.98	787.43	791.89	796.36	800.84	805.34	809.86

Appendix B

Resources You'll Use

For emergency road service and other membership benefits:

American Automobile Association
1000 AAA Drive
Heathrow, FL 32746
(800) AAA-HELP (222-4357)

To obtain an owner's manual for your vehicle:

Helm, Inc.
PO Box 07130
Detroit, MI 48207

They also supply other out-of-date or hard-to-get manufacturer information sources, such as electrical system and shop service manuals.

To find the market value of your used car:

NADA Official Used Car Guide
8400 Westpark Drive
McLean, VA 22101
(800) 544-6232
(800) 523-3110 (VA)

For more information about your credit rights you can write to:

Federal Trade Commission
Credit Practices Division
601 Pennsylvania Avenue NW
Washington, D.C. 20580

Make a toll-free call to the National Highway Traffic Safety Administration in Washington, D.C., to check if the make and model you want has had a recall issued or for free safety information.

Auto Safety Hotline
(800) 424-9393 toll free
(202) 366-0123 in Washington, D.C.
(800) 424-9153 TTY for the hearing impaired
(202) 755-8919 in Washington, D.C., for the hearing impaired

If you have trouble getting through on the hotline, you can request a copy of the vehicle owners questionnaire by writing:

Auto Safety Hotline—NEF-11
NHTSA
400 7th Street SW
Washington, D.C. 20590

Help with any insurance question is just a toll-free phone call away. The National Insurance Consumers' Helpline will courteously field your questions and provide free information about auto, homeowners, and business insurance. Sponsored by three nonprofit organizations, the helpline offers no-obligation guidance 8 A.M. to 8 P.M., EST. Call toll free (800) 942-4242.

APPENDIX C

More Resources—
Free or Cheap

BUYING A CAR:

FREE: For the consumer information catalog, write to Consumer Information Catalog, U.S. Government Printing Office, Pueblo, CO 81009.

FREE: The "New Car Buying Guide" is available from the Public Reference, Federal Trade Commission, Washington, D.C. 20580.

FREE: Order Ford's "Car and Truck Buying Made Easier," PO Box 1967, Southgate, MI 48195-9947.

CHEAP: The U.S. General Services Administration offers "Buying a Used Car," a 50-cent booklet available by writing R. Woods, Consumer Information Center-X, PO Box 100, Pueblo, CO 81002.

FREE: Brochures titled "Shopping for a Safer Car," "Injury and Collision Loss Experience," and "Report on Auto Theft" are available from the Insurance Institute for Highway Safety, 1005 North Glebe Road, Arlington, VA 22201.

FREE: "Buying a Used Car" can be ordered from Public Reference, Federal Trade Commission, Washington, D.C. 20580.

FREE: For information on federal government vehicle auctions contact the U.S. General Services Administration office in your area. Their number is listed in the telephone directory under United States government offices.

FREE: For monthly brochures on drug forfeiture auctions write Ernst and Associates Auctioneers, PO Box 3251, Modesto, CA 95353. For information on forfeiture auctions in your area check the Yellow Pages for auctioneers, or call the National Auctioneer's Association at (913) 541-8084.

FREE: Write for free consumer brochures on warranties and service contracts from Public Reference, Federal Trade Commission, Washington, D.C. 20580.

TIRES:

FREE: For "How to Take Care of Your Tires," write Goodyear Tire and Rubber Company, Public Affairs Division, Department 798, 1144 E. Market Street, Akron, OH 44316-0001.

FREE: Order "Tire Tips to Keep You Rolling" from Bridgestone, PO Box 140991, Nashville, TN 37214-0991, or call (800) TIRE-BSA.

FREE: "Weather from Behind the Wheel" is available from Michelin Tire Corp. Retail stores and local branches of the American Red Cross can provide.

CHEAP: A consumer tire guide and a kit that includes an air pressure gauge, tread depth gauge, four tire valve caps, and a plastic pouch is available for $4. Send check or money order to Tire Industry Safety Council, PO Box 1801, Washington, D.C. 20013.

CHEAP: The "Who Makes It? and Where?" directory is available for $5.50 including postage from Tire Guide, 1101-6 S. Rogers Circle, Boca Raton, FL 33487.

SAFETY AND ACCIDENTS:

FREE: A free list of federally approved child safety seats and booster seats is available by sending a stamped, self-addressed business-size envelope to Safe Ride Program at the American Academy of Pediatrics, PO Box 927, Elk Grove Village, IL 60009-0927.

FREE: A copy of the study "Effects of Cellular Phone Use Upon Driver Attention" is available by writing AAA Foundation for Traffic Safety, 1730 M Street, Suite 401, Washington, D.C. 20036.

CHEAP: The Center of Auto Safety information packets on a specific model's safety and repair history are available for $1 each. Send a self-addressed, stamped envelope with the make, model, and year of the requested vehicle to The Center of Auto Safety, 2001 S Street NW, Room 410, Washington, D.C. 20009.

CHEAP: The Accident Preparedness Kit is available for $29.95, plus $2 for shipping. Order from Elbros Products, PO Box 1923, Studio City, CA 91614.

CHEAP: For a free brochure on the Accident Pack write Bill Cumley, 1842 Caramay Way, Sacramento, CA 95818. Accident pack is available for $14.95, plus $2 for shipping and handling.

MISCELLANEOUS:

FREE: For a copy of the National Institute for Automotive Service Excellence's "Choosing the Right Repair Shop for Your Vehicle" brochure, send a self-addressed, stamped business envelope to ASE, Department DLC, 13505 Dulles Technology Drive, Herndon, VA 22071.

FREE: To receive the Insurance Information Institute's brochures, "Nine Ways to Lower Your Auto Insurance Costs" and "Oops: Common Questions About Auto Insurance," call (800) 942-4242.

CHEAP: The U.S. General Service Administration offers a 50-cent booklet on gas-saving products and practical efficient driving tips. Write R. Woods, Consumer Information Center-X, PO Box 100, Pueblo, CO 81002.

FREE: For "The Most Asked Questions About Motor Oil," write Norm Hudecki, Valvoline, PO Box 8797, St. Louis, MO 63102.

FREE: For a copy of the Magnuson-Moss legislation, write Allied Aftermarket Division, Fram/Magnuson-Moss, 105 Pawtucket Avenue, East Providence, RI 02916.

CHEAP: The U.S. General Services Administration offers "Car Rental Guide" with tips on renting a car. The 50-cent booklet is available by writing R. Woods, Consumer Information Center-X, PO Box 100, Pueblo, CO 81002.

FREE: The Federal Trade Commission offers a "Consumer Guide to Vehicle Leasing" brochure. Write Public Reference, Federal Trade Commission, Washington, D.C. 20580.

Appendix D

Auto Company Addresses

Alfa Romeo Distributors of North America
8259 Exchange Drive
Orlando, FL 32859-8026

BMW of North America, Inc.
300 Chestnut Ridge Road
Woodcliff Lake, NJ 07675

Chrysler Corporation
12000 Chrysler Drive
Highland Park, MI 48288

Daihatsu
4422 Corporate Center Drive
Los Alamitos, CA 90720

Fiat Auto U.S.A., Inc.
777 Terrace Avenue
Hasbrouck Heights, NJ 07604

Ford Motor Company
The American Road
Dearborn, MI 48121

General Motors Corporation
General Motors Building
Detroit, MI 48202

American Honda Motor Company
100 West Alondra Boulevard
Gardena, CA 90247

Hyundai Motor America
7373 Hunt Avenue
Garden Grove, CA 92642

American Isuzu Motors, Inc.
2300 Pellisier Place
Whittier, CA 90601

Jaguar Cars, Inc.
600 Willow Tree Road
Leonia, NJ 07605

Lotus Cars U.S.A., Inc.
1655 Lakes Parkway
Lawrenceville, GA 30243

Maserati Automobiles, Inc.
1501 Caton Avenue
Baltimore, MD 21227

Mazda (North America), Inc.
1444 McGaw Avenue
Irvine, CA 92714

Mercedes-Benz
1 Mercedes Drive
Montvale, NJ 07645

Mitsubishi of America, Inc.
6400 Katella Avenue
Cypress, CA 90630

Nissan Motor Corp. in U.S.A.
18501 S. Figueroa Street
Carson, CA 90248

Peugeot Motors of America
1 Peugeot Plaza
Lyndhurst, NJ 07071

Porsche Cars North America
One West Liberty Street
Reno, NV 89501

Range Rover of North America, Inc.
4390 Parliament Place
Lanham, MD 20706

Renault USA Corporate Group
100 Sylvan Avenue
Englewood Cliffs, NJ 07632

Rolls-Royce Motor Cars, Inc.
120 Chubb Avenue
Lyndhurst, NJ 07071

Saab-Scania of America, Inc.
Saab Drive, PO Box 697
Orange, CT 06477

Sterling Motor Cars
8300 N.W. 53rd Street, Suite 200
Miami, FL 33166

Subaru of America, Inc.
PO Box 6000
Cherry Hill, NJ 08034-6000

American Suzuki Motor Corporation
3251 E. Imperial Highway
Brea, CA 92621-6722

Toyota Motors Sales-USA
19001 S. Western Avenue
Torrance, CA 90509

Volkswagen of America, Inc.
888 West Big Beaver Road
Troy, MI 48007-3951

Volvo North American Corporation
Seven Volvo Drive
Rockleigh, NJ 07647

Yugo America, Inc.
28 Park Way
Upper Saddle River, NJ 07458

Appendix E

National and Local Consumer Groups

Consumers Union
256 Washington Street
Mount Vernon, NY 10553

Center for Auto Safety
2001 S Street NW, Suite 410
Washington, D.C. 20009

Consumer Federation of America (CFA)
1424 16th Street NW, Suite 604
Washington, D.C. 20036

Automobile Protection Association (APA)
PO Box 117
Station E
Montreal 151
Quebec, Canada

Consumer Education and Protective Association (CEPA)
6048 Ogontz Avenue
Philadelphia, PA 19141

Consumer Action
26 Seventh Avenue
San Francisco, CA 94103

Automobile Club of Missouri
201 Progress Parkway
Maryland Heights, MO 63040

Motor Voters
1350 Beverly Road
McLean, VA 22101

Aid for Lemon Owners is a consumer group that assists car owners with auto arbitration proceedings. Write: Aid for Lemon Owners, 21711 West Ten Mile Road, Suite 210, Southfield, MI 48075.

Appendix F

Industry Public Relations Groups

Motor Vehicle Manufacturers Association (MVMA)
7430 Second Avenue, Suite 300
Detroit, MI 48202

Automobile Importers of America, Inc. (AIA)
1725 Jefferson Davis Highway, Suite 1002
Arlington, VA 22202

Tire Industry Safety Council
844 National Press Building
Washington, D.C. 20045

Rubber Manufacturers' Association (RMA)
1400 K Street NW
Washington, D.C. 20005

National Automobile Dealers Association (NADA)
8400 Westpark Drive
McLean, VA 22101

Insurance Institute for Highway Safety (IIHS)
1005 N. Glebe Road, Suite 800
Arlington, VA 22201

Appendix G

Regulatory Agencies

Safety-Related Automobile Defects:

National Highway Traffic Safety Administration
Department of Transportation
400 Seventh Street SW
Washington, D.C. 20590
(800) 424-9393 toll free nationally
(202) 366-0123 in Washington, D.C.
(800) 424-9153 TTY toll free nationally, for the hearing impaired
(202) 755-8919 in Washington, D.C., for the hearing impaired

Proposing a new safety feature for automobiles:

Administrator
National Highway Traffic Safety Administration
Washington, D.C. 20590

Complaints on Warranty Service:

Warranty Project
Bureau of Consumer Protection
Federal Trade Commission
Washington, D.C. 20580

AUTO REPAIR PROBLEMS NOT CONNECTED WITH THE WARRANTY:

Consumer Subcommittee
Committee on Commerce, Science, and Transportation
U.S. Senate
Washington, D.C. 20510

Subcommittee on Telecommunications, Consumer Protection, and Finance
Committee on Energy and Commerce
U.S. House of Representatives
Washington, D.C. 20515

Director
Division of Consumer Affairs
Department of Transportation
Washington, D.C. 20590

Director
Office of Consumer Affairs
Department of Health and Human Resources
Washington, D.C. 20201

Bureau of Consumer Protection
Federal Trade Commission
Washington, D.C. 20580

Complaints about service stations in general or in particular can be brought to the attention of:

National Congress of Petroleum Retailers
2021 K Street NW
Washington, D.C. 20006

Repair Shop Problems

Director of Consumer Affairs
Office of Consumer Affairs
Office of the President
Washington, D.C. 20506

TIRE PROBLEMS

Tire Safety

> Administrator
> National Highway Traffic Safety Administration
> Washington, D.C. 20590

DECEPTION AND FRAUD IN THE PURCHASE OF YOUR AUTOMOBILE:

If you have been the victim of any sort of deception or fraud in purchasing a new car:

> Chairman
> Federal Trade Commission
> Washington, D.C. 20580

To complain about defects in the vehicle emission control system:

> Director
> Office of Mobile Sources
> Environmental Protection Agency
> Washington, D.C. 20460

APPENDIX H

Arbitration Program Addresses

Ford Consumer Appeals Board
Manager, Owner Relations Operations
Ford Motor Company
PO Box 1805
Dearborn, MI 48121
(800) 392-9292

Chrysler Customer Arbitration Board
Box 1919
Detroit, MI 48288
(800) 992-1997

Better Business Bureau
Contact your local BBB
or
Council of Better Business Bureaus
4200 Wilson Blvd., Suite 800
Arlington, VA 22203
(703) 276-0100

Autosolve
American Automobile Association (AAA)
Contact your local AAA
or

1000 AAA Drive
Heathrow, FL 32746
(407) 444-7740

Autocap
8400 Westpark Drive
McLean, VA 22102
(703) 821-7144

If you need legal assistance with your repair problem, the Center for
Auto Safety has compiled a list of lawyers who specialize in helping
consumers with auto repair problems. For a copy send a stamped,
self-addressed envelope to:

Center for Auto Safety
2001 S Street NW
Washington, D.C. 20009

Collecting the Money
Counsel for Courts Excellence
1024 Vermont Avenue NW, Suite 510
Washington, D.C. 20005

Everybody's Guide to Small Claims
by Ralph Warner (1987)
Nolo Press
950 Parker Street
Berkeley, CA 94710

Guide to Small Claims
Montgomery County Office of Consumer Affairs
100 Maryland Avenue
Rockville, MD 20850

Inexpensive Justice: Self-Representation in the Small Claims Court
by Robert L. Spurrier, Jr. (1983)
Associated Faculty Press, Inc.
New York, NY

Small Claims Court
Halt
Memberships Department
1319 F Street NW, Suite 300
Washington, D.C. 20004
Send $6.95

Index

Page numbers in **boldface**
refer to illustrations.

ABOUT THE AUTHOR

Lisa Murr Chapman is a founder of Motorcars of Brentwood, an automobile dealership serving the needs of discerning buyers of preowned autos in the Middle Tennessee area. Ms. Chapman launched the business in order to make stylish, dependable, affordable cars readily available, while helping to empower women in the automobile world. Prior to this venture, she was the founder, chairwoman, president, and CEO of a healthcare business in Nashville that grew to over $10 million in annual revenues with eight offices in five states by 1992. Ms. Chapman's professional awards and achievements include *Nashville Business Journal*'s Small Business of the Year and Executive of the Year finalist awards, as well as inclusion in *Nashville Business & Lifestyle* magazine's list of "40 under 40—Nashville's Emerging Leadership." Her business background includes seven years in sales and marketing, as well as six years in a variety of accounting capacities. Ms. Chapman received her MBA from the University of Houston.